WINE

AND · WINE · BASED

Cocktails

PARRAGON

ACKNOWLEDGMENTS

Archivio IGDA 33 top, 38, 70; Anthony Blake 14-15, 17 top left, 19, 30-31, 36, 45 top, 65 right; Cape Wine Centre 68-69; Colman's of Norwich Wines 67; Daily Telegraph Colour Library 50; Food & Wine from France 15, 17 centre; Fotobank International Colour Library 34, 37, 39 bottom, 46-47, 66, 71, 72; Robert Harding Picture Library 13, 49 bottom; Éd. Hespérides 40; Michael Holford 33 bottom, 35, 76 bottom; Michael Holford/ Gerry Clyde 42-43, 51, 52-53; Michael Holford/Stella Martin 56-57; Picturepoint 55, 57, 60, 65 left, 76 top; Spectrum Colour Library 75; Zefa 17 top right, 17 bottom, 39 top, 40-41, 45 bottom, 49 top, 59, 61, 63.

Special photography by Martin Brigdale (cover, 1-11, 20-21, 22, 23, 25, 26-27) and Paul Williams (78-93).

The Publishers would like to thank H. Sichel and Sons Limited for their assistance with wine for photography.

First published in 1984
by Orbis Publishing Ltd, London

This edition published 1994 by
Parragon Book Service Ltd
Avonbridge Industrial Estate
Atlantic Road, Avonmouth
Bristol BS11 9QD

© 1984 Orbis Publishing Ltd

Printed and bound in Hong Kong

CONTENTS

INTRODUCTION

A lot of nonsense is talked about wine, probably because all tasting is subjective and the elusive taste of a wine is particularly difficult to define. There are few precise tasting descriptions on which we all agree, so in the attempt to pin down a flavour, the imagination can run riot with all kinds of exotic adjectives and comparisons. Essentially, all you should really worry about is drawing the cork to provide a wonderful drink that will add an extra dimension to whatever you are eating. Wine transforms any meal – even simple bread and cheese takes on unsuspected qualities. With some rare exceptions (eggs and pickles are hardly ever good with any wine) it does not really matter what you drink with what. We all know the adage that white wine goes with fish and red wine with meat, but there is no reason why you should not drink red wine with fish if you prefer to. What is more important is to know *why* you like your fish with red wine. In other words the more you learn about wine the better you will enjoy it.

If you take the trouble to find out even a little about this fascinating subject, you will see the most modest bottle of wine in a new light. No one can ever know everything there is to know about wine. For one thing, it changes continually. With each new vintage there is something new to consider. Each bottle of wine is in its own way a surprise. True, the label can hint at what to expect; but will the wine live up to expectations, or exceed them? Labels alone cannot reveal the wine – happily, only drinking it can do that. Each time you try a new wine you will add to your cumulative knowledge and experience, and if you have taken the trouble to find out a little about the wine as well, your appreciation of it will be enhanced. Gradually you learn what to look for when choosing a bottle of wine; that is what this book is designed to help you do. And with knowledge comes confidence.

Wine drinkers in Britain are incredibly lucky, for the choice of wines in this country is enormous, and as a country that produces very little wine we are not subject to any of the regional chauvinism that exists in, say, France. (For example, it is not recommended to ask for claret in the heart of Burgundy.) Every wine-producing country sends its wines to Britain and the average wine shop or supermarket can offer bottles not only from France, Germany and Italy, but also from Chile, Australia, Bulgaria, America and so on, allowing us to enjoy wines from all over the world.

Surprisingly, as a nation we have a reputation as wine lovers. In a recent edition, the leading French newspaper *Le Figaro* quoted a market survey which concluded that the average Englishman was much better informed about wine than the average Frenchman.

Even a simple meal of bread and cheese is enhanced by a glass of wine. Learning a little more about the subject will help you enjoy wine still further.

HOW TO TASTE WINE

There is no mystery to tasting wine. If you can tell the difference between lamb and pork or thyme and chives, there is no reason why you cannot develop a palate for wine and learn the difference between wines made from the Chardonnay and Sauvignon or Riesling and Gewürztraminer grapes, for example. It is not a talent that you are born with, but a skill that can be learnt. The key is memory. With practice and experience you can develop and train your memory to recognize smells and tastes.

The problem is that, for most of us, our senses of smell and taste are undeveloped. In early youth we are taught to consider what we see and hear, to enjoy art or music, but it is considered almost self-indulgent to discuss what we are putting in our mouths. Consequently we do not really think about the reaction of our taste buds to the subtle differences of flavour.

As all tasting is subjective, there are very few basic yardsticks to judge a precise flavour and very few specific words in the English language to describe taste. Consequently an elaborate vocabulary of tasting terminology has evolved, usually evoking comparisons with flowers and fruits and sometimes more far-fetched allusions. For example, the late André Simon, one of Britain's most eminent wine writers, once described a Chablis as having 'the grace of weeping willow' and a particularly fine claret 'the magnificence of a copper beech'. The imagery may be startling, but it is illuminating. Because tasting involves subjective comparisons, even two people may not always agree. For instance, the smell of a particular grape variety may remind one person of blackcurrants and another of the cedarwood of cigar boxes. In fact both are perfectly acceptable ways of describing the bouquet of a fine claret.

Although the taste components in a mouthful of wine are numerous, the tongue only registers four elements of taste: sweetness at the tip of the tongue, sourness on the sides, bitterness at the back and saltiness in the middle. But there is more to tasting than just the tongue. First of all you have to look at a wine, and then you must smell it, before you can appreciate the full taste.

COLOUR

You can tell a lot about a wine from its appearance. First, a wine should always be bright and clear. A haze in a wine is an indication that something is wrong, unless it is an old bottle of red wine, in which a heavy, coloured deposit has formed and which has been shaken before opening. A white wine can vary

Three white wines (from the left, Bernkastel, Niersteiner Auslese and Sauternes) showing the progression from pale to deep yellow which often goes with increasing age or sweetness.

in colour between a very pale, almost watery greeny yellow such as you can find with a Muscadet, and the deep yellow, almost amber, of an old Sauternes or Trockenbeerenauslese. Usually a pale straw yellow will indicate a young wine with a crisp dry

The best way to assess the clarity and colour of a wine is to tilt the glass away from you, viewing the wine against a light background.

acidity, light in body and weight. As a white wine ages, its colour deepens, and if it is browning and tarnished, this is a warning sign that the wine is too old. Sweet white wines will also be a rich golden colour, but sometimes the golden hue may be an indication of age rather than sugar.

With red wines, the colour is a very important guide to the age of the wine, for as a red wine ages, it loses its youthful purple or ruby red colour and gradually develops a brick red or orange colour on its rim. The best way to see the colour of a wine is to tilt your glass against a white background such as a white tablecloth or a sheet of white paper; this will enable you to see the gentle gradation of colour. Lighting is also important; daylight is best whereas candlelight and fluorescent light often make wines look older than they really are.

The *depth* of colour is also important in red wine. A former wine-maker at one of the greatest French vineyards, Château Lafite, once said that the first duty of a red wine is to be red. But there is an immense variation in depth of colour. A heavy concentrated red will probably be a wine with a lot of body and weight, whereas a lighter red will usually be more elegant and less heady and tannic in taste.

The light, cherry red of the Chambertin (far left) and the purple red of the Beaujolais contrast with the fuller, richer red of the Bordeaux (second from the right). As red wine ages it develops an orangey, brick red colour at the edge, shown here in the 1976 Hermitage (far right).

You may also notice a glycerine-like streaking on the inside of your glass. This is what is poetically referred to as the 'tears' or 'legs' of a wine and it comes from the alcohol. It gives some clue as to the wine's strength. In other words, the more 'legs', the greater the alcohol content.

BOUQUET

The sense of smell is vital to tasting. Have you ever tried swallowing a mouthful of wine while you are holding your nose? You will find that you cannot taste a thing. It is the same as when you have a cold. The smell, or to use a tasting term, the 'nose' or bouquet of a wine can almost tell you more about it than the taste. In blind tasting, when you do not see the label on the bottle, the impression on the nose is more important than any other aspect.

The best way to smell a wine is to hold your glass by its base and gently rotate it for a few seconds, to enable the wine to give off its aromas. Take a short, sharp sniff. There is no need to inhale deeply. It is interesting to compare the difference between the intensity of smell you can get if you simply sniff your wine without moving it, and that you receive if you rotate it gently, or shake it vigorously – preferably putting your hand over your glass first!

What do you smell when you sniff a glass of wine? First, the wine should smell clean; that is to say, not of cork, or of vinegar, but the sharp or fruity flavour of wine. More experienced tasters will immediately receive from the smell a clue as to the origins of the wine, if they are tasting it blind, i.e. if the bottle is not identified. If they already know its origins, they will be able to judge its quality even more accurately. Is it a very fleeting bouquet, or is it pronounced and obvious? Does the wine smell fresh and fruity or is it old and tired; has it the developed bouquet of a mature wine or the youthful stalkiness of a young wine? Does it give you a prickling sensation at the back of the

To smell wine, hold the glass by its base and swirl the contents gently for a few seconds, then take a short, concentrated sniff.

nose? If so there is probably too much sulphur dioxide in it. Does it smell of oak, the rich vanilla flavour of Rioja or the more elegant cedarwood of fine Bordeaux? These are some of the things your nose may tell you. Occasionally you can come across a wine that hardly smells of anything at all, which makes it very difficult to identify.

FLAVOUR

Finally you come to taste the wine. Although the tongue only registers four primary tastes, you will in fact find out much more about the wine than that. Most important of all, you will discover whether you like it or not. Impressions of the nose should be confirmed by the palate. If you thought the wine smelt of a particular grape variety, it is reassuring to find that it also tastes of the same grape.

This is how you taste. Take a small mouthful of wine. Swill it round your mouth, while sucking in a little air at the same time and making sure that the wine covers every part of your tongue. Although this procedure sounds inelegant it does make sense. If you take in a little air as you taste, this enables the wine to give off maximum flavour and since different parts of the tongue register different tastes, it is essential that the wine comes into contact with all of them, otherwise you might miss something. Unless you are trying out lots of wines, there is no need to spit. Professional wine tasters spit out the wines because they could not drink all the wines at a tasting and remain sober. In any event, swallowing the wine will not tell them anything more about it than they could learn from holding the wine in their mouths.

Acidity is important in all wine, though more obviously in white wine. There should be the right amount, not so much as to be eye-watering and not so little as to be flabby and uninteresting. Acidity is one of the components in a wine that enables it to age, and it will lessen as the wine matures.

In red wines tannin is more obvious. A very young claret or a Rhône wine that has been aged in wood will have a considerable amount of tannin, coming from the grape skins and pips, and the oak barrels in which it has been stored before bottling. The sensation in the mouth is like that of drinking very strong tea, a puckering, drying feeling around the gums. As the wine ages, the tannin will gradually mellow and soften.

Sweetness may also be a factor. The tongue registers sugar and ideally it should be balanced with the acidity, so as not to be too cloying.

Most important of all is fruit. It is the basic flavour of the wine that makes it an enjoyable drink and fills out the mouth with flavour. A wine may have the right proportions of alcohol and tannin and acidity, but without fruit and flavour it is nothing. It is the fruit that comes from the combination of the grape and soil that gives a wine its individual character and its variations of flavour. The better a wine is, the longer that flavour will remain in the mouth after the wine has been swallowed. This is referred to as the 'finish', and the longer it lasts the better. With some wines of lesser quality, the flavour can suddenly stop as the wine is swallowed. A short finish is a disappointing sensation.

Alcohol is, of course, an important constituent of which you will be aware soon enough once you have drunk any quantity of wine. As far as the flavour is concerned, it is alcohol which gives weight and body to a wine. Compare a Moselle to a Châteauneuf-du-Pape. The Moselle is light, with about 9° of alcohol; the Châteauneuf-du-Pape, with a minimum alcohol level of 13.5°, is heady and full bodied and fills the mouth with flavour.

Attempts to describe a wine are fraught with hazard, as each description can only be personal and comparisons can only be made with other fruits or flowers, or whatever takes the imagination. However, it really is worth making the effort to write tasting notes for the wines you try. It may seem demanding at the time, but it helps you to remember what you have tried and whether you liked it and why, and with the discipline of finding appropriate descriptions, it concentrates your attention on the wine and helps you to acquire a 'taste memory'. Gradually you will find that you develop associations and adjectives that help you recognize a particular aroma or flavour. Some of the expressions most commonly used in the wine trade may help you to come to grips with the wine you drink. These are given in the glossary on page 94.

When tasting a wine you should only take a small mouthful, letting a little air into the mouth at the same time. Then pass the wine over as much of your tongue as possible before swallowing it.

SOME PROBLEMS AND FAULTS WITH WINE

One of the commonest complaints is of little pieces of what appear to be glass or sugar crystals at the bottom of the bottle. These are tartrate crystals formed from the wine's natural tartaric acid. If the wine has been left in a very cold place for a few days, perhaps in an unheated warehouse during the winter or forgotten in the fridge, the tartaric acid will form crystals. When this happens there is absolutely nothing wrong with the wine and the taste is not affected, nor will the crystals harm you. In some ways it is not a bad sign, as it indicates that the wine has not been excessively treated before it was bottled. All that needs to be done is to pour out the wine carefully so as to leave the crystals in the bottle.

Another so-called fault is the sediment that may be found in a bottle of red wine. Again, this is a perfectly natural phenomenon. As they age, red wines with a deep colour, like Bordeaux or vintage port, tend to lose some of their colour and leave a muddy deposit at the bottom of the bottle. Assuming that the bottle has been lying on its side, all that is necessary is to stand it upright for 24 hours to allow the sediment to settle. Then decant carefully, leaving the sediment at the bottom.

What are the serious faults we may encounter? Wine is a natural substance that is continuously developing and changing. Vinegar and wine are related, and wine which has been carelessly made or mistreated will turn acid and vinegary. This will be apparent from the smell. Don't drink it but do take it back to your wine merchant and claim a refund.

A sensitive nose is a great asset in recognizing a faulty wine, for the smell is usually the first warning that a bottle is corky. This does not mean that there are pieces of cork floating in the glass, but that the taste of the wine has been tainted by a bad cork. The wine will smell rather musty and all its fruit will dry up on the palate. This is not the fault of the wine-maker; it is just bad luck with a faulty cork and can happen to any wine, cheap or expensive. Fortunately these days it is a rare occurrence.

Finally you may come across a wine that is oxidized or 'maderized'. Both terms mean more or less the same thing. It happens when a wine is badly made, or too old with a white wine that is not meant to be aged, or with a bottle of wine that has been left open and exposed to the air. A very unpleasant smell develops and a white wine acquires a slightly tarnished colour and loses its brightness.

You may have accepted out-of-condition wine in the past, partly because you did not realize that there was something wrong with the bottle, and partly because you were too embarrassed or lacking the confidence to question its quality. Today's standards of production mean a faulty bottle is fairly rare, but if you do have serious doubts about a bottle of wine it is best to take it back to your wine merchant or, if you are in a restaurant, to query it with the wine waiter.

FROM GRAPE TO BOTTLE

The definition of wine, in simplified terms, is the product obtained exclusively from the alcoholic fermentation of fresh grapes. While wines can be made from certain fruits, flowers, vegetables and cereals, these are not wines in the proper sense. In other words, true wine comes only from grapes.

The alcoholic fermentation which turns the grape juice into wine is a perfectly natural phenomenon. When the grapes are pressed, the yeasts in the natural bloom of the grape attack the sugar in the juice and transform it into alcohol and carbon dioxide, and thus make wine. The fermentation process stops of its own accord when there is no sugar left and the alcoholic environment is too great for the yeast, so that it dies.

Although the origins of wine were probably Middle Eastern, it is now very much a part of European culture, having been brought to Europe by the Greeks and spread by the Romans, ultimately to be appreciated in other parts of the world that have been influenced by the European way of life.

Vines grow successfully only between certain latitudes, 50°N–33°N, in the northern hemisphere (in other words between southern England and North Africa) and between 23°S–40°S in the southern hemisphere, to include New Zealand and parts of Australia, South Africa and South America. The basic principles of wine-making are identical everywhere and yet within the world's vineyards there is the most enormous variety of tastes and types.

Wine has been known in Greece since 2000 B.C. There is still an air of antiquity about these terraced vineyards on the Isle of Samos, which produce a sweet, golden muscat.

Four essential elements determine the taste of a wine: the grape variety, the soil, the weather and finally the human element, the man who determines how the wine is made. Within these four factors there is an infinite variety of permutations and possibilities.

Specific details about grape varieties will be given in the section on the world's wines (see pages 30–69), but in general terms the grape variety gives certain basic characteristics and flavours to a wine which will be altered by the soil in which it is grown.

Inevitably, like any other plant, some grape varieties are much better suited to some soils than to others. In regions where there is a long history of wine-making, tradition and experience have long since revealed these tendencies so that no one, for instance, would consider planting Pinot Noir, the grape of Burgundy, in Bordeaux.

Generally, the poorer the soil is, the better the results, for the vine needs to struggle for survival. It has to be, as the Americans say, stressed and its roots go deep into the ground in search of nutrients and minerals. For these reasons many vineyards are on steep, stony hillsides where nothing else will grow. Vines on fertile plains produce exuberant vegetation but uninteresting grapes. A vine is at its peak of production at about 15 years old and, generally, older vines tend to make more interesting wine as they have developed a deeper root system.

The annual variations, those elements that determine the character of the vintage, come from the weather. In southern Europe or North Africa the variations are minimal, but in most parts of France there are considerable climatic differences each year which will determine the quality and quantity of a wine.

Vines need a certain amount of sunshine and warm weather to produce ripe grapes; less-than-ripe grapes will make wines high in acidity and low in alcohol. If there is too much rain, the crop will be diluted and excessive; too little, and the crop may be

rich and concentrated but also rather small. It may be easier to grow grapes in a country assured of constant sunshine, but the results are infinitely less interesting than those where there is more variation in weather. In some years the results will be less successful, whereas other years they will be excellent because of the ideal weather conditions.

In the northern hemisphere, a vine begins to grow in the spring when the temperature of the air reaches about 10°C (50°F), usually during March. It is undesirable for the buds to appear too early when there is still a danger of spring frosts, for then the vines could be damaged and the crop affected. The most important moment in the vine's cycle is the flowering which usually occurs during June. This is the moment when the tiny bunches of grapes, which are already formed, are germinated and the size of the crop determined. Bad weather, rain and cold will adversely affect the flowering, and the ideal is a period of warm sunshine. From then on warm summer sunshine with a little, but not too much, rain is hoped for. A wet summer will cause rotten and unhealthy grapes whereas a heavy rainfall just before the harvest can swell the grapes. Rain during the harvest can also cause rot and possibly dilute the resulting wine.

Spraying acres of vines with sulphur to protect them against mildew is made easier by the increasing use of mechanization (below) but many tasks must still be carefully performed by hand. (Left) Pruning a young vine at Anjou on the Loire valley.

At the harvest, the fourth factor comes into play – the wine-maker. He is presented with grapes of a certain quality from a vineyard that he knows intimately, and it is up to him to make the best possible wine from those grapes. A talented wine-maker will succeed in producing something acceptable from poor grapes. An unconscientious or inexperienced wine-maker can ruin an excellent crop.

White wine

What does the wine-maker do? Let us take the white wine first, for although the basic principle is the same, there is a different method for making red wine. After the grapes are picked, they are pressed with a gentle press that will not crush the pips (if the pips were crushed they would release too much tannin). The stems of the bunches may or may not have been removed first. The resulting juice, or 'must' as it is called, is first allowed to clarify, so that any large lumps of sediment, perhaps leaves or even stones, fall to the bottom of the vat. They are removed, and then the first fermentation can start. The natural yeasts from the bloom on the grape skins begin to work on the sugar in the must, turning it into alcohol and carbon dioxide.

Particular care must be taken over contact with oxygen. A certain exposure to the air does not do any harm and indeed may be necessary in some instances, but if there is too much, the white wine will quickly lose its fresh fruitiness and deteriorate. Consequently white wine is always fermented in closed vats, and often in stainless steel or enamel-lined concrete vats or some other inert material, rather than in oak barrels. However, some very fine white wine, such as great Burgundy and Sauternes, is fermented in oak barrels.

Temperature is of enormous significance during the fermentation, for the yeasts will only work between about 10–30°C (50–86°F). If the fermentation stops because the temperature goes below or above these temperatures, it is very difficult to get it going again and the ultimate quality of the wine will have been adversely affected. In hot climates many wine-makers favour cool fermentations for their white wine, although the virtue of these may be questionable in the loss of character in the wine, which may well be fresh and clean, but also unexciting. About 15°C (60°F) is probably the most desirable temperature and well-equipped cellars have the facilities to maintain this temperature.

Yeasts will naturally die when all the sugar in the must has been converted into alcohol or when they are overcome by the high alcoholic atmosphere. This happens when the alcohol level has reached about 15° but depends on the type of yeast. Some have a better resistance to alcohol than others.

After the first, alcoholic, fermentation comes the malolactic fermentation, when the malic acid (as in apples) is transformed

(Top left) Everyone hopes for sunshine in September when, in about the third week, the harvest begins. (Top right) Rich red wine of the Côte d'Or in Burgundy being pumped into a chilled tank to begin its second fermentation. (Centre) The ageing process begins in barrels in the cellar. (Above) The maître de chai *draws off a sample of wine with a probe, to test its development.*

into lactic acid (as in milk). This either happens immediately after the first fermentation or may not occur until the following spring when the weather is warm again. This phenomenon reduces the acidity in the wine and is still not completely understood. As recently as 30 years ago, it was thought that the wine was acting in sympathy with the sap rising in the vines in the spring.

Once the alcoholic and malolactic fermentations have taken place, the wine has to be finished. Finer white wines will often be aged, either in oak or in the vat for some months, or even a year or two, before they are bottled. Wines for early consumption in youthful freshness will have to be clarified, that is, fined to remove the larger sediments and filtered to remove the finer sediments and also possibly tartrates. The presence of tartrate crystals in wine has already been discussed on page 12 but they can be avoided. More sophisticated wineries with expensive machinery can refrigerate their wine so that the tartrates precipitate and can be filtered out of the wine. In this way they will have no problems once the wine is bottled. Other wine-makers are content to let this happen naturally over the winter months, which may not be quite as efficient, but is less traumatic for the wine.

Once the wine is star-bright, it is ready for bottling. The sophistication of the bottling machine depends on the size of the winery and includes everything from a tiny manual machine to the huge and fully automatic bottling hall where no bottle is touched by human hand and many thousands of bottles an hour are processed.

For sweet wine there are slight variations on the theme. The best sweet wines (Sauternes and finer German wines, for example) are made from over-ripe grapes that have been attacked by a particular fungus (*Botrytis cinerea*) which does not rot them, but concentrates their juice to an almost raisin-like sweetness. This phenomenon is called 'noble rot'. There is no way that the yeast can ferment out all the sugar in this type of grape juice until it is dry, so luscious sweet wines are the result. These wines are, however, very special and the noble rot requires particular climatic conditions which by no means occur every year.

More commonplace sweet wines can be made by stopping the fermentation at the desired level of sweetness. Sulphur dioxide is added to kill the yeasts which can then be filtered out of the wine. In northern areas it can be a problem to obtain fully ripe grapes that will produce sufficient alcohol. If there is not enough sugar in the grapes, the resulting wine, be it sweet or dry, will be thin and lacking in body and alcohol. Consequently a process called chaptalization is permitted. Dr Chaptal introduced the process in the nineteenth century in which sugar beet is added to the grape must in order to give the yeasts extra sugar to be transformed into alcohol. If used carefully it is a perfectly acceptable way of turning an indifferent wine into a good one,

Tasting the wine: an expert consults his notes

by giving it a better balance and more body. This process is used mainly in northern France and is strictly forbidden in the South of France, Italy and other Mediterranean countries.

In Germany, on the other hand, they use what is called *Sussreserve* to sweeten their wines. This is unfermented grape juice with all the yeasts removed which is added to a newly made wine. It is a sophisticated way of giving what would otherwise be a light acid wine, lacking in fruit, considerably more character. You only have to compare a Trocken (with no *Sussreserve*) to a Kabinett wine (with *Sussreserve*) from the same vineyard, to see exactly how desirable this addition can be. The Kabinett wine has infinitely more character and flavour. In the same way, many English wines would benefit from the use of *Sussreserve*.

ROSÉ

The methods for making rosé wines are almost identical to those for whites, except that the must remains on the grape skins at the beginning of the fermentation for as long as is necessary for the wine to absorb the required amount of colour.

RED WINE

It is often forgotten that the juice of red grapes is white. The colour of red wine comes from the grape skins, and so one of the most significant factors in red wine-making is the length of time the juice spends with the grape skins.

Basically the principles for making red wine are the same as white. The grapes, with or without their stalks, are pressed and the fermentation starts. The temperature is generally warmer than that for white wine, and may be as high as 24°C (75°F) so that as much colour and tannin as necessary is extracted. Red wine is usually fermented in open-top stainless-steel vats. However, more traditional growers may still use large wooden vats and press the grapes by foot. Newer vats have a paddle to circulate the skins through the juice, or sometimes the skins may just form a kind of covering or *chapeau* ('hat' in French) over the fermenting must. The must will be run off the skins once the desired amount of colour has been absorbed and the fermentation will continue until the yeasts are exhausted.

As with white wine, malolactic fermentation then takes place and chaptalization may be permitted. However, maturation of the wine before bottling is usually more significant than that for white – there are few red wines that are sold within the year of the vintage. Obvious exceptions are Beaujolais *nouveau* and the other so-called 'new' wines following the trend (Côtes du Rhône *nouveau* or the Italian *Vino novello*), but generally most red wine has some ageing, either in vat or in barrel, before it is bottled. The process may take from a few months to five or six years, depending on the region.

Oak ageing is of considerable importance for fine red wines, such as the great Bordeaux and Burgundies. It is considered that the natural aromas in this kind of wine develop better in wood than in a steel vat. The wood itself gives complementary aromas to the wine and the wine tends to clarify naturally.

BLENDING

Blending can be a significant factor in wine-making. Bordeaux is an obvious example of this, when each grape variety in the vineyard is vinified separately and blended, usually in the spring after the vintage, in proportions determined by the wine-maker. It is then allowed to harmonize in the barrel. In other areas, several grape varieties are fermented together as they arrive in the cellars.

POURING AND STORING

There is no need for complicated equipment in order to enjoy wine – a glass and a corkscrew are all you need. But having said that, it is perhaps worth considering the presentation of the wine. As with food, a little extra care and attention can make all the difference, just as a garnish enhances a soup, so an attractive glass can increase the pleasure of the wine.

GLASSES

Wine glasses come in all shapes and sizes and even colours, so which are best? Coloured glass can be dismissed immediately. It can be very pretty but useless if you want to see the colour of your wine. So what are the basic requirements of a good wine glass? First, size: you need a substantial glass that enables you to pour out a generous measure without overfilling the glass. There is nothing worse than the tiny glass filled to the brim that makes it absolutely impossible for you to 'nose' your wine, because if

A sherry copita (left) is ideal for fortified wine, while the Paris goblet and the 'tulip' suit almost any wine. Serve champagne in a flûte (right).

you attempt to rotate the glass the wine will spill. A glass should be filled to about two-thirds full, never to the brim, so that the wine can be gently savoured. Those glasses which have a slightly incurving rim help to concentrate the bouquet. A clear glass – rather than, say, a crystal – allows you to appreciate the wine's colour without distortion. And this, after all, is one of the great pleasures of drinking wine.

A tulip-shaped glass is ideal if you do not want different glasses for different wines. It is equally suitable for red and white wine, still or sparkling. There is no reason for wine of a different colour to call for glasses of a different shape. Tradition used to dictate that champagne should be drunk out of flat, saucer-like glasses. In fact, one could not devise a glass less suitable for champagne as the bubbles disappear rather quickly with such a large surface area of wine. If you want to keep the sparkle in your champagne for as long as possible, use the tall and elegant *flûte*.

It may seem obvious, but it is also too often forgotten that the glass must be absolutely clean and not have any smell of, for instance, detergent or a musty cupboard, as this again will ruin the wine. Smeared glasses also detract from the wine's appearance.

CLEANING GLASSES

To clean glasses, soak them in very hot water, the hotter the better. It is best to avoid using detergent, but if you do, rinse the glasses thoroughly afterwards. Then wipe off the excess water with one cloth and polish with another. If the glass is hot, it is much easier to dry and polish and it will not be smeared.

To warm a glass of red wine that has been served too cold, cup the bowl of the glass in your hand (below). White wine, however, is usually served chilled (right), so avoid warming it inadvertently by holding the stem of the glass.

TEMPERATURE

The temperature of a wine affects its taste enormously so it is worth taking the trouble to serve it correctly. Most white wines should be chilled: an hour or two in the fridge is quite sufficient. If the wine is too cold, the flavour is numbed and you might just as well be drinking frozen alcoholic water for all you can taste. However, if it is not cold enough, a white wine tends to taste rather flabby and lacks bite.

Traditionally, red wines are served at room temperature (*chambré*) but that was before the days of central heating. The average room today is generally too hot. Think rather of the temperature of an unheated room, say about 15°C (60°F).

So what do you do if you have got the temperature wrong? A white wine will warm up very quickly if you cup your glass in your hands, and for this reason it is always best to hold the wine glass by the stem, rather than by the bowl, to avoid making your wine turn tepid. If you need to chill quickly a bottle of white wine that is not cold enough, 15 minutes in a freezer should be sufficient. This cannot be recommended for a fine white wine, but for an everyday bottle, it should not do any harm.

If a red wine is too cold, cup the filled glass in your hands to take the chill off it. More drastic measures such as standing the bottle near a fire or radiator or in a saucepan of hot water are not recommended, as you are likely to end up mulling the wine, and that is another story.

If a red wine is too warm, it will also taste flabby. Indeed, Beaujolais is better drunk slightly chilled, and so are some other similar reds, Gamays from other parts of France, Italian Lambrusco, and other sparkling reds. Even full-bodied reds in a hot climate taste much better slightly chilled.

DECANTING

The other important decision when serving wine is whether to keep the wine in its bottle or pour it into a carafe or decanter. For white wines there is nothing at all to be gained from doing this, but a mature red wine, such as a claret or port, may have thrown a lot of sediment at the bottom of the bottle, and this wine will be worth decanting. The bottle should be stood upright for 24 hours to allow all the sediment to fall to the bottom. The wine should then be carefully poured into a decanter. If you place a light or a candle under the neck of the bottle, you will see the sediment coming up with the wine and accordingly know when to stop pouring. You should, depending on how much sediment there is, have about ½-1in (12-25mm) of wine left at the bottom of the bottle.

At the other end of the scale, even though it should not have any sediment, a simple *vin rouge* or *vino rosso* can benefit from the airing it is given by decanting for even the most basic wine will mellow a little in contact with air.

How long should a bottle of wine be opened before it is served? It varies according to the wine. It can vary so much from wine to wine, from vintage to vintage of the same wine even, that there are really no hard and fast rules. Wine will develop when in contact with fresh air; the problem is to get the right balance – too little and the wine may still be all closed up and too much may spoil the wine, especially if it is from an old bottle and therefore more fragile. Generally, a white wine does not need to be opened in advance. A red wine of medium age and good quality will probably need to be opened a couple of hours beforehand. But, of course, it is often a matter of circumstance. There is no point in saying a bottle should be opened three or four hours beforehand, when you do not get home from work until 6.30 pm and your friends are coming around at 7.30 pm. In any case a good wine will develop considerably in the glass, especially if the wine is swirled to air it.

STORING

'Laying down' wine for drinking in the medium or long term will need a different kind of storage facility from wines which you have bought for immediate, everyday drinking. Given that most of us live in a cellarless house or a flat that is centrally heated, where should you keep your precious bottles?

There are three things that are particularly detrimental to wine – light, heat and vibration. Light will harm all wine. It must be kept in darkness or it is likely to develop a haze and deteriorate. And for the same reason, avoid buying bottles of wine that have been directly exposed to light on a wine merchant's or supermarket's shelves for long periods of time.

The ideal temperature for storing wine is between 7–13°C (45–55°F). However, it is better to have a slightly higher constant temperature of nearer 15°C (60°F) than considerable seasonal fluctuations. Wines kept at a slightly higher temperature will tend to develop a little quicker than those kept in a very cold atmosphere. If the temperature is much over 15°C, the effect is one of a steady cooking process, and must be avoided at all costs.

A wine that has been constantly moved or shaken will never show its best qualities. In the same way, a wine needs to be rested after a journey. Do not, for instance, drink a bottle of good wine just brought back from a holiday abroad.

So, where is the best place to keep your wine? The essentials are cool and dark. Some people favour a cupboard under the stairs, but these tend to be rather overheated and have the additional problem of vibrations from footsteps pounding overhead. The attic or the garage are other possibilities, but they are both subject to temperature fluctuations. A cupboard in an unheated room is best if you have not got a cellar. Wherever is chosen, a wine bottle should always be stored on its side so that the cork is kept moist and therefore airtight. A dry cork will allow air into the bottle and cause the wine to deteriorate.

So much for storing wine . But which wines should be laid to mature for several months or even years? Not every wine is worth keeping, and many are best drunk in early youth. It is difficult to generalize about this, but a few guidelines are possible.

Wine should always be kept on its side, so that the cork stays moist and airtight. A cool, dark cupboard is ideal for storage.

LAYING DOWN

Laying down is a kind of investment for future drinking, buying a wine when it is first offered in its early years and forgetting about it for a few years, trying a bottle or two and then drinking it when it is at the peak of perfection for your taste. However, not all wine is worth laying down. It may be perfectly delicious if drunk now, but will not improve in the bottle (indeed some, like Beaujolais *nouveau*, are intended to be drunk early).

Most white wines on the average wine merchant's shelves are meant for immediate drinking. Many, such as Muscadet or Soave are best drunk young when they are fresh and fruity. It is true that some white wines age well, but these are the more expensive and rarer wines, such as Sauternes, German Beerenauslese, and white Burgundies such as Chablis and Meursault.

Red wines and port are the main candidates for laying down, but here again not all red wines benefit from bottle age. The average Valpolicella, Rioja or Beaujolais is ready for drinking the moment it arrives in this country. A red wine which will age well must have a lot of tannin when it is young. The tannin creates a puckering sensation around the gums and this will fade as the wine matures. Not only must there be tannin, but also a balancing amount of fruit, acidity and flavour. A deep colour is also a good sign.

Red wines to lay down might include Bordeaux, Burgundy, port, Rhônes and some from northern Italy (Barolo, for example). These are all wines that benefit from a considerable amount of bottle age and which are not only very expensive to buy when they are mature, but also difficult to find by that time.

READING THE LABEL

The label on the bottle should tell you a great deal about the contents. In the first place a well designed label is the eyecatcher that makes you pick out that bottle on the supermarket shelf. An unattractive label will probably leave the bottle standing unnoticed. Label styles very enormously and, like advertising, depend upon the impression or image the wine conveys – perhaps a classic, sober Bordeaux, or a jolly *vin de pays*, or a Germanic Liebfraumilch.

The amount of writing on labels can vary greatly from wine to wine. The wine label should tell you exactly what you are buying but, depending upon the category of the wine, there is compulsory and optional information to be included.

TABLE WINE

The label must tell you that it is table wine (in France this is *vin de table*, in Germany *Tafelwein* and in Italy *vino da tavola*) and give its country of origin, but otherwise no further information need be given (although if you know your French postal codes, these can give you some clues; for example, 21600 is Beaune in Burgundy and 33000 is Bordeaux). There must always be the name and head office address of what is officially called 'the responsible bottler'. This may be the producer or the company that has imported the wine.

Look out also for blended wines from more than one EEC country. There are wine labels that look very colourful and Germanic, with the appropriate Gothic script which, on closer examination, show that the wine is not really German, but probably 'Germanized' Italian wine that has had a small amount of German wine added and was bottled in Germany. Read the small print carefully and look out for the words 'Blend of wines from different countries of the European Community'.

Finally, the quantity. Since Britain joined the EEC quantities have become much more uniform, and nowadays the standard bottle size is 70 or 75 centilitres. Gradually, the 70 centilitre bottle will disappear.

In addition to the compulsory information, there are various pieces of optional information that are allowed on a wine label, such as a brand name and the colour of the wine. The alcoholic content may also be given, expressed as a percentage volume such as 12% or 12°. And there may be an indication of whether the wine is sweet or dry or any variation in between.

VIN DE PAYS

The next stage up the quality scale is table wine with a geographical origin, what in France is called a *vin de pays*, in Germany a *Landwein* and in Italy a *vino tipico*. Confusingly, these wines must also say 'table wine' in the respective language on the label, although they are better than basic table wine. As well as the same obligatory information on the label, there is a wider choice of optional information, such as the geographical area of origin or even a vineyard name, a grape variety and a vintage. There may be bottling terms such as *mis en bouteille à la propriété* (bottled at the property) or *imbottigliato della cantina sociale* (bottled by the cooperative). The use of terms like *château, domaine* or *castello* is closely controlled and can only be used if the wine really does come only from that vineyard and is made solely at that property. A *château* is not necessarily a large mansion. Information about the history of the vineyard and advice on how the wine should be served is also allowed.

QUALITY WINE

The final category is quality wine. Here the precise category of quality must be stated, as well as the country and area of origin. So for France we have *Appellation Contrôlée* (AC) and *Vin Délimité de Qualité Supérieure* (VDQS); in Italy *Denominazione di Origine Controllata* (DOC) and *Denominazione di Origine Controllata e Garantita* (DOCG); and in Germany there is *Qualitätswein bestimmter Anbangebiete* (QbA) and, at a higher level *Qualitätswein mit Prädikat* (QmP) (of which there are five, in ascending order of sweetness: Kabinett, Spätlese, Auslese, Beerenauslese and Trockenbeerenauslese.)

In addition, all sorts of optional information is allowed: vintage, alcoholic strength, grape varieties, advice on how to serve the wine, colour, vineyard name, shipper's name, its history and ageing, method of production, and other supplementary description. These may also be what are called 'traditional descriptions' which cover an enormous variety of different terms. Most common amongst the French ones are expressions like *premier* (or *1er*) *cru* and *grand cru* which refer to the quality of the wine within its *appellation*.

In Italy *riserva* and *riserva speciale* refer to the time the wine has been aged before sale, which varies from region to region. *Classico* indicates that the wine comes from the heart of the region. *Superiore*, like the French *supérieur*, indicates that the wine has a higher alcoholic content than table wine.

Bottling terms tell you whether the wine was bottled at the place of production, by the proprietor or in a co-operative cellar: *mis(e) en bouteille à la propriété* or *mis(e) d'origine*; *Erzeugerabfüllung*; *imbottigliato dal viticoltore, imbottigliato all'origine, imbottigliato dalla cantina sociale*.

Quality wine

FRANCE

- Name of the property where the grapes were grown and the wine was made
- Médoc is the name of an area in Bordeaux producing fine wine. Pauillac is a town within the Médoc
- Vintage: the year in which the grapes were harvested. 1981 was a good year for the Médoc
- Name of the vineyard near Pauillac
- One of the major wine-growing areas of France
- This means 'bottled on the estate' and is a sign of quality.
- A guarantee that the wine was produced in Pauillac
- Local society supervising standards
- Amount of wine in bottle

GERMANY

- Region in Germany where wine was produced
- Year of harvest; 1976 was a good year for Rüdesheim
- Rüdesheim is a town on the Rhine famous for its vineyards
- Name of estate
- Variety of grape
- Degree of sweetness: late-gathered with high sweetness rating
- Indication of top quality. The number is that of the *Prädikat* (certificate) granted to the wine
- Name of shipper
- Amount of wine in bottle (50 ml less than the French and Italian examples shown here)

ITALY

- Trade name; name of grower
- Type of wine. One of the best Italian reds
- Equivalent to the French *Appellation Contrôlée;* an indication of quality, though less reliable than French or German controls
- Made and bottled in the area in which the grapes were grown
- Name of producer
- Region of Italy producing the best known and most reliable wines
- Serve with care at 20—22°C (70°F) i.e. room temperature

WINES OF THE WORLD

This concise survey is intended to give a general idea of the character of the wines of each country, with an indication of which we may find on a local wine merchant's shelves. Inevitably there are many omissions from less important areas.

FRANCE

We begin with France as she continues to hold her position as the largest exporter of wine to Britain, and many still think of French wines before those of any other country. There are two crucial events in the development of French wine.

The first, the arrival from America in the middle of the nineteenth century of a small but pernicious vine pest – phylloxera, caused considerable destruction. Phylloxera was first found in the South of France in the early 1860s, and within 30 years it had spread all over France as well as elsewhere in Europe. Its effect was devastating. Phylloxera attacks the roots of the vine, which then gradually dies. After many experiments, a remedy was eventually discovered – the grafting of the European vines on to American vine roots, which are resistant to phylloxera.

Château Ausone overlooks the valley of the River Dordogne.

The other milestone was the culmination of the *appellation contrôlée* wine laws in 1935. In general terms these laws lay down the regulations for each wine and cover grape varieties, soil types, methods of cultivation and the permitted yield. The regulations also define the precise area of production. These laws have gradually been extended to include three other lower categories, in descending order: *Vin Délimité de Qualité Supérieure* (VDQS), *vin de pays* and basic *vin de table*. VDQS is the smallest category, and is seen by some as an inferior *appellation contrôlée* that may even eventually disappear.

Vin de pays is a relatively new and growing category that first appeared in 1973. Most *vin de pays* comes from the South of France, but can be found all over the country. The object was to give the better table wines the distinction of a geographical definition, albeit a very large one, to raise them above the ordinary anonymous table wine.

River systems, which were vital for transport in the Middle Ages, have played a vital part in the development of the French vineyards, and so it is by river that we shall cover the vineyards of France.

LOIRE   Variety is the essence of Loire wines. They are mainly white, sweet as well as dry, sparkling as well as still and there is also a little red and some rosé.

Travelling downstream, the first important vineyards we come to are those of Sancerre and Pouilly Fumé, where the white Sauvignon grape makes deliciously mouth-watering wines, characterized by adjectives such as smoky, gooseberry, and

some say flinty. Nearby there are the similar but less well-known wines of Reuilly, Quincy and Ménétou-Salon. Although these are the main *appellations* for the Sauvignon grape, it is grown along most of the Loire valley. Sauvignon de Touraine is an attractive and cheaper alternative to Sancerre and the picturesque-sounding Sauvignon de la Jardin de France is an attractive *vin de pays*. This central region of the Loire also produces a little red and rosé wine, most notably in Sancerre, from the Pinot Noir grape.

Further downstream we come to Vouvray, a small village on the north bank of the river. Vouvray can be dry or sweet and anything in between, as well as still, *pétillant* (very slightly sparkling) or sparkling. It is made from the Chenin Blanc grape that grows successfully on the chalky soil of the area. The best Vouvrays have a lovely honeyed character.

Moving westwards past elegant châteaux we come to the region of Anjou which is perhaps the most diverse of all the Loire wine areas, for here are red, rosé and sparkling wines, as well as a variety of whites. The sparkling wines will be dealt with on page 70. Anjou is the area for some of France's greatest sweet wines, second only to the Sauternes of Bordeaux. In the valley of the river Layon, a tributary of the Loire, the Chenin Blanc grapes are often affected by 'noble rot'. As explained on page 18 this is a fungus that attacks grapes when they are almost ripe. It flourishes when moist and humid conditions are followed by warm autumn sunshine. The affected grape turns raisin-like and its juice becomes rich and concentrated, producing a luscious and sweet wine. Coteaux du Layon is the most common of all the sweet Loire wines, but there are two smaller and more outstanding areas – Bonnezeaux and Quart de Chaume.

One of the most individual of all Loire wines comes from Savennières. Here again the Chenin Blanc is the grape variety, and it makes a wine that is neither sweet nor dry, but with a characteristic individuality. Coulée de Serrant and La Roche aux Moines are the two main names within the *appellation*.

It is not possible to talk about the wines of Anjou without mentioning Anjou Rosé. Made from a blend of grapes, it is pretty and pink with a touch of sweetness. Cabernet d'Anjou, made purely from the Cabernet Franc grape, is also pink and slightly sweet and is considered to be one of France's best rosé wines. There are also the equivalent appellations in white, Anjou Blanc, and in red, Anjou Rouge. In the same way, Saumur gives its name to red, white and pink wines.

Anjou also makes some of the best red wines of the Loire valley, from the Cabernet Franc grape. The names to look out for are Chinon, Bourgueil and, even more distinctive, St Nicolas de Bourgeuil.

The wine of Brittany, on the Atlantic seaboard, is Muscadet, named after the white grape of the same name. Forty years ago this wine was virtually unknown outside its own locality, but

(Above) The Loire valley is one of the most attractive regions of France, as these curving terraces near Beaulieu-sur-Layon bear witness. Cabernet and Chenin Blanc grapes are grown here, producing wines that are smooth without cloying, easy to drink without food. (Left) Loire vines like a long warm autumn to give of their best at harvest.

today is one of the best-known dry white wines of France. With its crisp fresh acidity, it is generally considered to be an ideal accompaniment to seafood.

BORDEAUX Travelling south, but keeping to the Atlantic coast, we come to the city of Bordeaux in the *département* (the equivalent of a county in England) of the Gironde. This is the home of some of France's greatest wines, both red and sweet white, where thousands of individual châteaux produce wines of every category and quality from *premier grand cru* to a simple *appellation contrôlée*. The term 'claret' is often applied to the red wines of this region but is not a term used by the French. It dates from the substantial English involvement in the Bordeaux wine trade during the late Middle Ages, which persists even today.

The geography and vineyards of Bordeaux are also determined by its rivers – the vast estuary of the Gironde, fed by the

Garonne and the Dordogne. There are several *appellations* within the region, although in some ways they can be divided very simply. The Médoc (with the villages of St Estèphe, Pauillac, Margaux and St Julien – and, less important, Listrac and Moulis) is on the left bank of the Gironde. St Emilion and Pomerol are the right bank, and Graves is to the south of the city of Bordeaux. Then there are satellite *appellations*, such as Côtes de Bourg and Côtes de Blaye on the right bank of the Gironde and, further inland, Côtes de Castillon and Côtes de Canon Fronsac.

The predominant grape variety throughout Bordeaux is Cabernet Sauvignon, which is blended mainly with Cabernet Franc and Merlot grapes. The mix can vary with each individual château, but in general terms there is more Cabernet Sauvignon in the Médoc and Graves, making a more austere wine, and more Merlot in St Emilion and Pomerol to make a richer, more rounded wine. Most red Bordeaux is aged in oak for some months.

In 1855 the main châteaux of the Médoc, plus Haut Brion from the Graves, were classified into five categories, or *crus*, according to their quality and importance. Their cost matches their reputation, however, and wine enthusiasts of modest means should look to the peripheral areas of Bordeaux for drinkable claret. Every wine merchant worth his salt has a carefully chosen selection of *petits châteaux*, with perhaps the *appellation* Médoc or Haut Médoc, right down to a simple *appellation* Bordeaux or 'house claret'. There are too many names to suggest, but it is these *petits châteaux* that give the great names of Bordeaux their solid base and provide lovers of claret with more accessible wines. Claret is undoubtedly one of France's finest wines; it is elegant and austere, with fruit and bite, and will age in bottle to develop unsuspected qualities.

WHITE BORDEAUX White wine-making techniques have improved enormously all over Europe in recent years and Bordeaux is no exception. These wines come from the Sauvignon grape and are not dissimilar to those produced on the Loire. They are usually found as Bordeaux Blanc or Sauvignon Sec, or possibly under a château name. They will usually be in tall-shouldered green bottles; sweet wines are usually in clear glass bottles.

Some of the most famous wines of Bordeaux have been produced at Château Mouton-Rothschild for over a hundred years. (Left) The maître de chai *Raoul Blondin inspects the clarity of the new wine by candelight.*

(Above) Château Lafite-Rothschild is one of the largest vineyards in the Médoc, making one of the greatest – and most expensive – French wines.

A modern mechanical harvester at work, an increasingly common sight in the vineyards of France.

The greatest sweet white wines of France come from Bordeaux. As in the Loire they are the result of *pourriture noble* ('noble rot' – to be distinguished from destructive rot – *pourriture grise*), the fungus that has shrivelled the grapes and concentrated their juice. But this does not happen every year; the weather conditions must be right with the perfect combination of warmth and humidity. Heavy rain has spoilt many a potentially fine vintage, but when the weather is kind, the result is superlative among dessert wines. The yield, however, is always small. At Château d'Yquem, most famous of all the Sauternes châteaux, the grapes of one single vine yield enough juice for one small glass of wine. To say it is liquid gold is hardly an exaggeration.

The two main *appellations* for sweet wine are Sauternes and Barsac and there are neighbouring *appellations* such as Premières Côtes de Bordeaux and Ste Croix du Mont, that produce good but less distinguished sweet wines, that are less dependent on the vagaries of the climate.

Bordeaux also produces dry white wines. Best of all are those from the Graves, an area that makes both white and red wine, and some of its châteaux are equally well known for both. However, the mass of white Bordeaux comes from the Entre-Deux-Mers region which is so called because it is situated between the two tidal rivers of the Garonne and the Dordogne. Once these wines were neither dry nor sweet, but with the growing taste for dry white wines, producers have made their wines increasingly crisper.

SOUTH-WEST FRANCE   From the south west of Bordeaux down to the Pyrenees there are pockets of vines that are slowly being discovered as the wine trade seeks out alternatives to the increasingly expensive wines of Bordeaux and Burgundy. Those areas closest to Bordeaux, such as Bergerac and Côtes de Duras, follow very much in the footsteps of Bordeaux for their grape varieties and methods of production; those further afield such as Gaillac, Jurançon, and Cahors have their local traditions and peculiarities.

Bergerac is in the *département* of Périgord, perhaps better known as the Dordogne. Bergerac's problem is that it has been overshadowed by its larger and more important neighbour, Bordeaux. Until recently Bergerac red wine presented itself as a cheaper kind of claret, which it certainly is not, although the grape varieties are the same. It is a wine, or rather several different wines, with a very individual style. The other important change in the area is the switch to dry white wine. Ten or 20 years ago a lot of indifferent sweet white wine was made. Today there is a definite trend towards producing a dry Bergerac and there has been a dramatic improvement in production methods and quality of the wines of the area over the past decade or so. Today it is a region of enormous variety, with red, sweet white, dry white and even a little rosé and sparkling wine. The red and dry white are usually sold under the names of Bergerac Rouge and Blanc and the sweet as Monbazillac. Côtes de Duras, Côtes de Marmandais and Côtes de Buzet produce similar wines to Bergerac. Further afield there is Cahors, traditionally known as the 'black' wine of Cahors, from around the historic town on the river Lot. In fact, modern wine production has made its colour rather lighter. The grape variety is mainly the Auxerrois, a variety peculiar to the region, and it makes a wine that will age well. To the east Gaillac produces white wine from the rugged vineyards of the Gorges du Tarn. The vineyards of Jurançon at the foothills of the Pyrenees produce white wines that have a long history. Traditionally they were sweet but now more and more dry Jurançon is being made. The red wines of the Pyrenees are Madiran and Irouléguy, both full-bodied reds, produced from local grapes.

White wine from Meursault, on the Côte de Beaune, is invariably fine.

BURGUNDY Travelling from north to south, Chablis is the first vineyard of Burgundy, and is commonly called the 'Golden Gate' of Burgundy. Although it is closer to the vineyards of Champagne, commercially and historically it has always been linked with Burgundy. It is a small vineyard that gives its name to one of the best known of all white wines. There are four different *appellations*, in descending order: Chablis *grand cru* (with seven different vineyard names), Chablis *premier cru*, (with 12 different names), Chablis and, much less important, Petit Chablis. The grape variety is Chardonnay.

Some traditional growers still age their wine in wood, while others of more modern outlook use stainless steel and the results are crisp and steely. Traditionally Chablis is the ideal accompaniment to oysters – appropriately, as the vineyards grow on an ancient bed of oyster fossils.

Adjoining vineyards make less well-known, but excellent red wines, Coulanges-la-Vineuse and Irancy, that often prove better value than wines from further south in Burgundy. The village of St Bris grows the only Sauvignon to be found in Burgundy, a VDQS sold as Sauvignon de Saint Bris.

Further south we come right to the heart of Burgundy, to the town of Beaune. The greatest Burgundy comes from the Côte d'Or, the 'Golden Slope' that is divided into two areas: the Côte de Nuits and the Côte de Beaune. The Côte d'Or is the home of famous names such as Clos de Vougeot, Romanée-Conti and Mazis-Chambertin. More affordable are the basic village wines of the Côte d'Or, such as Pommard, Nuits-St-Georges, Beaune or Volnay. The Côte de Nuits makes predominantly red wine from the Pinot Noir grape. Some are great wines, made by traditional methods and aged in oak barrels in cool cellars. The red wines of the Côte de Beaune tend to be a little lighter, though both are elegant.

The great white Burgundies also come from the Côte de

(Left) The Pinot Noir grape makes the best red wine in the world, and is the only variety grown for red wine on the Côte d'Or.

(Above) *The Hospices de Beaune, endowed in the 15th century with vineyards that have maintained it to this day.*

(Top) *Spraying at Chablis, where one of the world's classic wines is grown.*

Beaune, from the Chardonnay grape. Corton-Charlemagne, Meursault and Puligny-Montrachet are some of the best. Here each vineyard is owned by a network of proprietors, so it is the name of the winemaker that is important in the choice of a wine. Prices tend to be high as the vineyards are so tiny and the quantities so small. Better value is often found from a little further south on the Côte Chalonnaise where the grapes and the wines are very similar. Four villages give their names to the *appellations* of the area, Givry and Mercurey for predominantly red wine; Rully for white and red, and Montagny for whites.

Further south still we come to the undulating hills of the Mâconnais and Beaujolais. Mâcon, with the most common *appellation* – Mâcon Villages – is best known for white wine, although the fruity, youthful Mâcon Rouge is also made. Pouilly-Fuissé and the adjoining *appellations* of Pouilly-Vinzelles and St Véran are sound whites (both from the Chardonnay grape.)

A local saying has it that Lyons is watered by three rivers, the Rhône, the Saône and the Beaujolais. The hills north of Lyons produce fruity red wine in copious quantities from the Gamay grape. Most of it is destined for early drinking, and Beaujolais *nouveau*, which is released every year on the 15 November (only about six weeks after the harvest) accounts for nearly half the production of all Beaujolais. Ideally it should be drunk by the end of the year. However, more serious Beaujolais comes from nine different communes: Fleurie, Moulin-à-Vent, Brouilly, Côtes de Brouilly, St Amour, Morgon, Juliénas, Chénas and Chiroubles. Here individual estates make more long-lasting Beaujolais that can develop unexpected and delicious characteristics in a good vintage such as 1978. Otherwise drink the youngest Beaujolais available.

(Below) Châteauneuf-du-Pape gives its name to one of the most powerful French wines, made from a blend of grapes including Syrah.

THE RHÔNE VALLEY South from Lyon flows the river Rhône. The wines of the Rhône valley can be divided, north and south, for very different grape varieties are grown and consequently different wines are made in each area. In the north, opposite the old Roman town of Vienne, are the steep terraced vineyards of the Côte Rôtie (literally, the 'roasted slope') with its Côte Brune and Côte Blonde, their names taken from the colour of their soil. Côte Rôtie is made from the Syrah grape and is aged in wood for several months. It is red, full-bodied and high in alcohol, rich and warming on a winter's night.

The white wines of the northern Rhône come from the Viognier grape, unique to this part of France. At Condrieu and at Château Grillet (the smallest appellation of France), it makes wonderful perfumed wines reminiscent of apricots. Then, moving on south we come to the vineyards of Hermitage and Crozes-Hermitage around the town of Tain l'Hermitage. These two *appellations* are predominantly red, full-bodied wines from the Syrah grape and the best are aged in oak for several months. Some white is made from two local grape varieties, Marsanne and Roussanne, but they are less important.

Across the Rhône there is more red wine at Cornas and St Joseph and white wine at St Péray, of which the sparkling version is more common than the still. Between Valence and Orange the countryside is scorched and infertile. Near Montélimar is the Coteaux du Tricastin, a relatively new vineyard. The majority of the growers here are from North Africa and have successfully applied Algerian methods in France. The grape

varieties are those of the south, and mainly red wine is made. A detour along the river Drôme, a tributary of the Rhône, produces Clairette de Die, a sparkling wine from around the town of Die (see page 72).

The southern Rhône is dominated by Châteauneuf-du-Pape; this was the wine drunk at the papal court of Avignon and it was for Châteauneuf-du-Pape that the first wine laws, forerunners of the *appellation contrôlée* laws, were devised. Today Châteauneuf-du-Pape can vary quite considerably in style depending on the wine-making methods and the proportions of the 13 different grape varieties that are permitted in the blend. Traditional methods favour a long fermentation and a lengthy ageing in wood, to produce wine that will keep for years. In contrast, more modern methods produce a lighter style of wine, but one still rich in flavour and alcohol, for at 13.5° Châteauneuf-du-Pape has one of the highest alcohol contents of any French wine. Some estates also make a much less common white version.

Around the vineyards of Châteauneuf there are other wines of similar character. Gigondas is a relatively new *appellation* not unlike Châteauneuf-du-Pape. There is Vacqueyras, one of the best of the Côtes-du-Rhône-Villages, so that it now has its own separate identity. There is also the mass of simple Côtes-du-Rhône, the basic and most common wine of the Rhône valley. Several villages make this warm, uncomplicated wine and some of them are allowed to include their name on the label.

This is also a region of rosé wine. The village of Tavel is reputed to produce the best in France and nearby is Lirac, better known for its red, although its rosé and white versions are also

good. Other uncomplicated reds from this part of France come from the Coteaux du Lubéron and the Côtes de Ventoux. Last but not least comes Muscat de Beaumes de Venise, a luscious dessert wine from the Muscat grape, and a wine that can compete even with Christmas pudding or mince pies.

THE MIDI Vines proliferate all along the Mediterranean. Yields can be enormous, but the wine is not always good, and is sometimes undrinkable. However, in recent years enormous advances have been made to improve the quality of the wines of the south. Yields and grape varieties are carefully controlled. The most usual red-wine grapes are Cinsault, Mourvedre, Carignan and Syrah and occasionally a little Cabernet Sauvignon can also be found. Today the Midi can produce some very drinkable wine at very affordable prices.

The region west of the Rhône estuary is known as Languedoc-Roussillon, which comprises four *départements*: the Gard, the Hérault, the Aude and the Pyrénées-Orientales. This is primarily a region of *vins de pays*, or country wines, the category of wine that was introduced with the object of improving the quality of the mass of anonymous table wine that was made in the Midi and to raise some of it above the basic level.

Vin de Pays du Gard, de l'Aude, d'Oc and so on are the most common wines, and there are also picturesque names. For example, who could resist a Vin de pays de la Vallée du Paradis or from the Ile de Beauté (Corsica)? Although there are *vins de*

The sun-baked vineyards of Provence in the south of France produce robust wines best drunk young.

pays all over France (the notable exceptions being Bordeaux, Burgundy and Alsace), it is in Languedoc-Roussillon that they really come into their own. A *vin de pays* from an individual estate where the wine-maker is good can offer excellent drinking value. Both red and white wines are made, but it is not too sweeping a generalization to say that the reds tend to be better than the whites. It is a question of acidity, which is vital in white-wine grapes, and sometimes lacking if the grapes are too ripe, with the result that the wine is flabby and lacks in bite.

Languedoc-Roussillon also has wines of higher status than *vins de pays*: Minervois, Corbières, Fitou and Costières du Gard, for example. The good ones are warm and fruity, although sadly they are sometimes rather unexciting. Listel is another name to look out for from the south. This is the brand name of a company called Les Salins du Midi who produce, as their name implies, salt as well as wine.

Provence, too, to the east of the Rhône estuary, produces wine amidst the olive groves and wild thyme. The best known of all, the rosé Côtes de Provence, is easily recognized by its distinctively shaped bottle. Côteaux d'Aix-en-Provence, from around the town of the same name, is often rosé, but can also be red – and often more successfully so.

ALSACE   Alsace, sadly, is often overlooked by wine drinkers. It is a region with distinct German characteristics (it was once a part of Germany) and is separated from the rest of France by the Vosges mountains. Its vineyards are a continuation of the German vineyards of the Rhine valley and, perhaps inevitably, Alsace wines share with German wines grape types not found elsewhere in France; but there the similarities end. Whereas the wine-makers of Germany aim for elegant sweet wines, those of Alsace want something more powerful, so the wines are fermented completely dry and are generally full and grapey with an underlying spiciness.

Unlike any other region of France, apart from Champagne, the wines of Alsace are labelled according to the grape type and precise vineyard and village names are unimportant.

Alsace is overwhelmingly a white wine region, relying on the Sylvaner, Pinot Blanc, Pinot Gris (or Tokay as it can be called in Alsace), Muscat, Riesling and Gewürztraminer. (In Alsace they consider their best wines to come from the Riesling grape; it produces a flowery wine with good acidity and body, delicious on its own or with a meal.) Where the grape variety is mentioned on the label, the wine is made from that grape alone, but some producers also make a blended wine – Edelzwicker – from a mixture of grape varieties. Each grape variety is quite distinctive. Sylvaner is perhaps the least interesting, light and grassy. Pinot Blanc is traditionally drunk in Alsace as an aperitif. Tokay has a slightly more spicy character; Muscat even more so and, most pungent and individual of all, is the Gewürztraminer (*Gewürz* means 'spice' in German).

(Above) Alsace is one of the prettiest wine-growing regions of France.

Long dry summers ripen the grapes for the vintage (below).

GERMANY

Every German wine is allocated a category, according to where it is grown and made and its sugar content, which determines its quality. German wines should be fragrant, elegant and flowery. The sweetest ones are honeyed but never sickly and heavy, for the high acidity gives them a refreshing lightness. All German wines of any quality are submitted for analysis and tasting and accordingly issued with a certificate. There are three basic categories:

Tafelwein, or table wine is the most common and the cheapest. It is usually a blend and may well include wine from other EEC countries. In this case the label should say so. If it says simply *Tafelwein*, the chances are that it is not native German, but a

Schloss Vollrads is one of the most venerable wine-producing estates on the finest wine land in Germany, the Rheingau.

Germanized Italian or French wine. These 'Euroblends' are often very misleadingly Germanic in their appearance, with the appropriate Gothic script and German-style bottle. Pure German table wine calls itself *Deutscher Tafelwein* and is produced in one of five large regions that together cover the whole of Germany. *Landwein* is more distinguished than *Tafelwein* and is designed to equate to the French *vin de pays*. It can come from one of 15 regions and is basically a superior table wine.

Qualitätswein is of a higher quality and is commonly referred to as QbA, the German abbreviation for quality wine of a specified region, of which there are 11 in Germany. It is worth remembering their names: Ahr, Baden, Franconia, Hessische Bergstrasse, Mittelrhein, Mosel-Saar-Ruwer, Nahe, Rheingau, Rheinhessen, Rheinpfalz (or Palatinate) and Württemberg. Each one of these areas is divided into *Bereiche*, or smaller districts, and within those there are village names, and then individual vineyards.

Qualitätswein mit Prädikat (often referred to as QmP) forms the highest grade. Prädikat wines are divided into five types according to their natural sugar levels, which may vary slightly from region to region. From driest to sweetest QmP wines are rated: Kabinett (having the minimum must weight), Spätlese (which literally means 'late picked'), Auslese (late gathered with a high natural sugar level), Beerenauslese (very sweet and luscious) and finally Trockenbeerenauslese, (from grapes that have dried on the vine, so that their juice is very sweet and concentrated).

Sweetness is an important factor in German wine. It is only in very good years that the richer Beerenauslese and Trockenbeerenauslese are made, as they depend purely on 'noble rot' to concentrate the grape juice and make a rich, luscious wine.

The most common of all German wines, Liebfraumilch, takes its name from the vineyards that surround a church, the Liebfraumenkirche, in the town of Worms in the Rheinhessen district. However, the name now has a much wider application. Originally Liebfraumilch was a blend of grapes from four regions of the Rhine, the Nahe, Rheingau, Rheinhessen and Rheinpfalz, but since 1982 any blending has been forbidden and the wine must come entirely from one of those four regions. Good Liebfraumilch should be light, fruity and only slightly sweet.

It is the Rhine and its tributaries that provide the link between the wine-producing areas of Germany, from the most northerly of the Ahr, just below Bonn, to the most southerly in Baden, and on down to the shores of Lake Constance. Germany has some of the most northerly vineyards of Europe, so climate is a crucial factor in the quality of her wines. Warm summers and long autumns are the ideal, and the best grape varieties are those that can stand the winter cold.

The finest German wines are made from the Riesling grape, while the more everyday ones come from the Müller-Thurgau. Silvaner (as in Alsace, although differently spelt) is now less important and there are a variety of new experimental crossings being developed for their frost-resistance and shorter ripening period, in an attempt to beat the weather.

Details of the seven main wine-exporting areas are as follows.

MOSEL-SAAR-RUWER   The river Mosel flows from Trier to Koblenz through some of the most beautiful of vineyard scenery. This region is the home of famous wines such as Piesporter Goldtröpfchen, Wehlener Sonnenuhr (German wine names are logical: Piesport and Wehlen are village names, Goldtröpfchen and Sonnenuhr are vineyard names), and the much esteemed and accordingly expensive Doktor vineyard at Bernkastel. These wines are the lightest and most fragrant of all German wines. A Mosel Auslese from a good vintage is a perfect delight on a summer's evening but a more simple Bereich Bernkastel would do almost as well.

(Above) In high summer wild plants soon shoot up to colour the vineyards.

(Below) Trimming long shoots from Riesling vines near Rudesheim.

Mechanical harvesting methods are particularly useful on vineyards as steeply terraced as these on the Mosel.

The areas around the Saar and Ruwer rivers are said to produce wine of a steelier, firmer quality than those of the Mittel Mosel (as opposed to the lower Mosel that flows through Luxembourg). Eitelsbach on the Ruwer and Ayl on the Saar are two particularly reputable villages.

RHEINGAU   Here is produced the greatest of all German wines, with such great estates as Schloss Vollrads, Schloss Johannisberg, and the Cistercian abbey of Kloster Eberbach.
The Rheingau runs from Rüdesheim to the suburbs of Wiesbaden and then to the east of Frankfurt where the village of Hochheim gives its name to the term Hock, by which all Rhine wines traditionally have been known.

NAHE   Nahe wines come from the valley of this Rhine tributary, and are a cross between the Mosel and the Rheingau. This is a small region, often overlooked, that makes light, spicy wines. Schloss Böckelheim produces some of the best-known wines.

RHEINHESSEN   Further south than Nahe, the wines are heavier and fuller than those of the Rheingau. Much of its production goes into Liebfraumilch, and other familiar names are Niersteiner Gutes Domtal and, from a wider area, Bereich Nierstein. Oppenheim is also important.

PALATINATE   As we go south the wines become heavier and I have even heard them described as clodhoppers. New and often

50

very perfumed grape varieties predominate in the southern Palatinate, although the villages of the northern part are the homes of some famous producers. The Palatinate is also responsible for large quantities of *trocken* (dry) and *halb trocken* (half-dry) wines.

FRANCONIA Franconia, on the river Main, has the picturesque town of Würzburg at its centre. It is famous for its Steinwein in characteristic flagon-shaped *Boxsbeutel*. Steinwein has a drier, more steely, quality than other German wines.

BADEN This is an area that has been coming into its own in recent years. With its warmer, southern climate, its production is more regular than that of the vineyards of the north and there is some good basic wine around at a reasonable price, mainly thanks to the co-operatives of small growers. The village names tend to be obscure, so look out for 'Baden' on the label.

Bacharach is a district at the northern end of the Rhine valley.

ITALY

It is hardly an exaggeration to say that Italy is one large vineyard, and indeed the Greek name for Italy was *Oenotria*, the land of the vine. Italian wine-making has improved enormously over the past 20 years or so, and the introduction of the Italian wine laws during the 1960s was partly responsible for this. The categories they created are: *vino da tavola* (table wine) which may have some indication of its origin (in which case it is called *vino tipico*), *Denominazione di Origine Controllata* (DOC), and *Denominazione di Origine Controllata e Garantita* (DOCG). This last category came into operation with the 1980 vintage and wines with this accolade are only now beginning to appear on our shelves. (At present there are four: Barolo and Barbaresco

San Gimignano in Tuscany overlooks Chianti vineyards in a landscape that has cast a spell over poets and painters for long centuries.

from Piedmont, Brunello di Montalcino and Vino Nobile di Montepulciano from Tuscany. Chianti Classico and Albana di Romagna will be added in the not-too-distant future.)

Since 1963 some 200 DOCs have been recognized. Some are well-known wines such as Soave and Valpolicella and others are more obscure wines such as Bianco Pisano di San Torpè, from Tuscany. However, Italians are individualists and some of their best wines do not conform to the DOC regulations. Two of Italy's most reputed wines, Tignanello and Sassicaia, have mere table wine status.

Classico on the label means that the wine comes from the heart of a particular region and *superiore* denotes an alcohol content of a degree or half a degree higher than that of the basic *appellation*.

From north to south, these are the main Italian wine areas.

PIEDMONT   Piedmont produces Italy's greatest wines from the
Nebbiolo grape, chief among them the heady Barolo and the
elegant Barbaresco. It is above all, with one important exception,
a region of oak-aged red wines. The exception is the sparkling
wine Asti Spumante (see page 73). There are three main wine
areas in Piedmont. Most important are the rolling hillsides
around the towns of Asti and Alba. Here the Nebbiolo grape
produces full-bodied, heavy wines. Barolo needs three years in
cask (four if it is to become Barolo *Riserva* and five to be Barolo
Riserva speciale). Barbaresco needs two years in cask. Other
grape varieties found in this area include Barbera, which is the
most common and comes in three forms, based on geographic
origins: Barbera d'Alba, d'Asti and del Monferrato, and Dolcet-
to, which is not, as its name might imply, at all sweet.
    In northern Piedmont in the Valle d'Aosta the vineyards in
the foothills of the Alps are some of the highest in Europe. Here
the Nebbiolo grape makes rich, full-bodied Carema and Donnaz
wines. Further east, in the Novara hills, Gattinara is the best
known wine (also from the Nebbiolo grape). There is also
Spanna, a local name for Nebbiolo, and a wine that does not
conform to the DOC regulations.

VENETO   This is the region between Lake Garda and the Vene-
tian lagoon. Three wines stand out above the others in popularity – two reds: Bardolino and Valpolicella, and a white – Soave.
However, they do not have the great stature of, say, Barolo, and
are best suited for casual drinking. Bardolino comes from the
pretty lakeside village of the same name and Valpolicella, which
is a fuller wine, from vineyards further inland from Lake Garda.
The vineyards of Soave surround the hilltop town with its
ruined castle.

TRENTINO-ALTO ADIGE   The Alto Adige prefers to call itself the
Südtirol, for it was once part of Austria, whereas the Trentino, in
contrast, is firmly Italian. Grape varieties are all-important here
for it is after these that the wines are named. Most commonly
found on sale in Britain are Cabernet (often a mixture of both
Franc and Sauvignon), Merlot, Pinot Bianco, Chardonnay, Pinot
Grigio, Riesling and Traminer Aromatico (or Gewürztraminer).
Although the influence is French as well as German, there are
also local vine varieties – a full-bodied Teroldego Rotaliano and
a fruity red Marzemino.

FRIULI-VENEZIA-GIULIA   This region is further east, bordering
Yugoslavia and here there are six DOCs, each based on an area,
and each including several grape varieties. Most common is
Grave del Friuli for which the main grapes are Cabernet (again
Franc and Sauvignon), Merlot, Pinot Bianco, Pinot Grigio, and
Tocai. Refosco is an indigenous red grape from which is made a
hearty, full-bodied wine.
    The whites from this area are generally fresh and fruity and

The vineyards of Trentino in north-east Italy early in the season. By winter, they may be covered with snow.

meant for early drinking – the younger the vintage the better. The reds, again, do not benefit from much ageing.

EMILIA-ROMAGNA Here is the land of table wine in which anonymous red Sangiovese and white Trebbiano grapes grow prolifically. Lambrusco comes from around the city of Modena. It is usually sweet, red and fizzy, but a dry version is also made.

TUSCANY Chianti is the region's most celebrated wine. Once bottled in wicker-covered flasks, it is now more commonly found in Bordeaux-style bottles. The Chianti area lies within a triangle formed by the cities of Siena, Arezzo and Florence. However, the heart of the area is around Greve, midway between Florence and Siena. This is Chianti Classico country, whose wines are identifiable by the distinctive black cockerel on the label on the neck of the bottle. There are two distinct styles of Chianti, the young fruity wines that can be very slightly fizzy and which should be drunk in early youth, and the fuller richer wines that are aged so that they are entitled to the word *Vecchio* (old) after two years and *Riserva* after three years' bottle age. Like Bordeaux this is a region of individual estates, and there are well over 200 producers, so the choice is enormous.

Carmignano is a small area adjoining Chianti that has only recently become a DOC, although it has a tradition almost as old as that of Chianti. The grape varieties are a similar mixture, with Sangiovese, one of Italy's most commonly grown vines, predominant. The difference is that a small amount of the Bordeaux grape, Cabernet Sauvignon, is used as well.

There are two other great Tuscan reds, and these have had DOCG status since 1980. Brunello di Montalcino is made from the Brunello grape, grown around the town of Montalcino. It is aged for a minimum of four years in wood, five if it is *Riserva*. Vine Nobile di Montepulciano needs two years in wood, three if it is to be *Riserva* and four for *Riserva speciale*.

At the other end of the scale – in that they are mere table wines – but comparable in quality to the DOCG wines, are Sassicaia and Tignanello. Both are aged in wood and come from one of the most famous of all Chianti producers, Antinori.

The regulations for Chianti insist on a small percentage of white grapes in the blend, but the modern school of thought favours the minimum possible, so with the surplus of white grapes a new white wine has appeared – Galestro, so called after the stones in the vineyard. It is a white table wine from the Tuscan hills and typical of the new modern vinification methods and improvements in Italian wine-making.

Another notable white wine from Tuscany is Vernaccia di San Gimignano, made from the Vernaccia grape around the picturesque town of San Gimignano with its many high towers.

UMBRIA A region reminiscent of Tuscany, Umbria – north of Rome – boasts mainly white wine, and in particular Orvieto. Traditionally Orvieto was *abboccato* (slightly sweet) rather than *secco* (dry) which is the version more common today. In fact, after Soave, this is Italy's most popular white wine. The other important DOC of Umbria is Torgiano, which has been pioneered by the Lungarotti family. The red is made from the same grapes as Chianti, and the white, often with more character than Orvieto, is called Torre di Giano. The family's experiments continue and theirs is a name to look out for.

THE MARCHES The most famous wine of this area is Verdicchio dei Castelli di Jesi, a crisp dry white wine made from the Verdicchio grape. It usually comes in an amphora-shaped bottle.

LATIUM To the north of Rome (the centre of the Latium region) there are few wines of distinction available outside the area.

To the south, however, are the vineyards of the best known white wine of the region – Frascati. Like Orvieto, Frascati was traditionally slightly sweet (*amabile*), but now tends to be dry, and is best drunk as young as possible.

MEZZOGIORNO Here in the South sunshine and vines are plentiful, and traditionally the wine was high in alcohol but low in quality, and suitable only for use as the base wine for aperitifs or for blending with lighter wines from other regions. However, there is now a gentle move towards quality. It is by no

(Left) In Italy, where vines have been cultivated throughout history, even small farms produce their own wine. (Above) Peace and order at Ascoli Piceno where Verdicchio is produced.

means uniform, but throughout southern Italy there are pockets of vineyards producing wines of note.

ABRUZZO   This area is mountainous and rugged and has a wine to match – Montepulciano d'Abruzzo, from the grape of the same name. There are three versions, a full-bodied red which is even better when aged for two years, a rosé called *Cerasuolo* for its cherry colour, and a complementary white, Trebbiano d'Abruzzo. Variations of the Trebbiano grape are found throughout Italy. Some say it grows like a weed and here it makes a dry full-flavoured wine.

CAMPANIA   Campania can boast one of the most picturesque of wine names, Lacrima Cristi del Vesuvio (Christ's Tears of Vesuvius). The vineyards lie along the southern slopes of the volcano, and red, white and rosé versions can be found. However, better but less common wines from Campania are two dry whites, Greco di Tufo and Fiano di Avellino and a distinctive red, Taurasi.

SARDINIA   This is a unique wine area, for many of its wines are made from grape varieties peculiar to the island. Among the best Sardinian wines is Torbato di Alghero (Torbato is the grape, Alghero the place) which is a dry, fresh, white wine, produced by a long established and highly successful company. For reds try Cannonau, rich, full and powerful. The Sardinians consider it to be their greatest red wine, but as the grape is grown all over the island and made into wine by a number of different producers, the style can vary. The basic version is dry and aged for a year in wood. *Riserva* denotes three years in wood.

SICILY   The island is best known for the fortified wine, Marsala. As for table wine, the best comes from producers whose wines, for one reason or another, are not accorded DOC status, but who have established reputations in their own right. Corvo is the most common in this country with sound red and white, and their methods are among the most modern on the island. Regaleali and Rapitalà are two other names to look out for. Finally, there is a sweet dessert wine, Moscato di Pantelleria which, as its name might suggest, is made from the Muscat grape on the tiny island of Pantelleria, closer to Africa than Italy.

SPAIN

Not so long ago, before Britain joined the EEC, Spanish wine was often found under somewhat camouflaged names such as Spanish Chablis, Spanish Burgundy and Spanish Sauternes. However after our entry these spurious allusions to French wines have disappeared and Spanish wines have reassumed their true individuality and identity.

RIOJA   This is the area producing what is now probably the best known of all Spanish wines, but has only really established its popular reputation over the last ten years. It comes from northern Spain, around the town of Logroño. The Río (river) Oja flows through the region, from which the wine takes its name. A mixture of grape varieties are grown. The reds can be aged in American oak for several years and have the characteristic flavour of vanilla. There is an indication of ageing time on the label. *Reserva* indicates a minimum of two years in wood and one year in bottle and *Gran Reserva* – made only in exceptional years – is aged in oak casks for a minimum of three years, with two years in bottle. Often these times are longer, depending on the style of the individual *bodegas* or producers.

White Riojas are sometimes aged in oak, although some producers are now making a fresher, fruitier white wine. This is an area that offers very good value for money, especially the reds, as they are often very reliable wines with a characteristic style, although some people may find the oak flavour a little overwhelming. Much more recent arrivals to this country are wines from the adjoining provinces of León and Navarre. They are similar to Rioja, but usually cheaper.

PENEDÉS   This region is second only to Rioja as a wine-producer. It is the home of Cava, the sparkling wine of Spain (see page 73), and of some excellent table wines.

Otherwise, apart from a few small but unimportant pockets of interesting vines, and of course sherry (see page 76), the rest of Spanish wine-making is unsophisticated and the wine forms part of that large anonymous lake of *tinto* and *blanco*.

Though they have only recently come to prominence in this country, the wines of Spain are excellent, particularly those from the Rioja region, where the estates have a long history.

PORTUGAL

Apart from port (see page 74) Mateus Rosé – the pink, slightly sparkling wine in the dumpy bottle is probably the best-known Portuguese wine. Mateus is one of the great commercial successes of the wine trade and has been imitated by other producers. It was first made in the 1940s, the brainchild of Fernando Guedes, and this grand old gentleman, now in his 80s, still runs the family company. Since 1982 a white version has also been made. Perhaps surprisingly it is not sparkling, but slightly sweet, light and fruity. Neither the pink nor the white Mateus come from a precise vineyard area; the Guedes family buy grapes from the peasant farmers all over northern Portugal.

The Minho area of northern Portugal is the home of Vinho Verde, the green wine, so called because it is best drunk young when it is very fresh. It also has a crisp, green acidity with a very slight, refreshing sparkle. The countryside of the Minho is also very green, and torrential rain is not uncommon. The vines grow in an unruly fashion on tall trellises and even up trees. There are none of the formal vineyards that one sees in France.

Dão is the great red wine of Portugal, although there is also a white version which tends to be rather heavy. The red is full-bodied with lots of flavour. It is at its best when it has been

The Palace of Vila Real in the Douro region in northern Portugal. It is here that the famous Mateus rosé is produced.

While modern methods are being introduced into winemaking all over Europe, in Portugal the old ways linger on.

opened for several hours and it really does need to be drunk with food. Older vintages can be found at very reasonable prices and offer incredibly good value for a mature wine, as do some of the other more obscure reds which can be found in this country. Periquita ('parrot') and Pasmados are two other wines worth seeking out as warming stylish reds.

ENGLAND

During the late 1970s in England there was an enormous growth in enthusiasm for vines and viticulture and there are now some 200 commercial vineyards in southern England and in Wales.

Of course, the problem with making English wine is the

weather. How often do we have a summer fine enough to ripen the grapes? Yet despite the vagaries of the climate, some producers make really excellent wine. The inexperience of many producers is another handicap. They are often enthusiastic amateurs with some spare land that is often not really suitable for vines, and their methods at first are a little haphazard. Also, most of the English vineyards are still very young, and there is no doubt that older vines generally produce better wine.

There are affinities between German and English wines in the grape varieties and climatic conditions, and those wine-makers who follow German methods are often the most successful. At Lamberhurst Priory in Kent, for example, the wine-maker is German and spends half his week at his vineyard in Baden and the other half at Lamberhurst. English wines are also criticized for their high price and, sadly, a comparable German wine is much cheaper. The main reason for this is the short-sighted policy of successive governments that continue to tax the home production at the same rate as any other wine from the EEC, whereas wine producers in other countries are given the advantage of paying negligible, if any, tax.

The most successful English wines carry a seal, EVA, an award from the English Vineyards Association, to indicate that they have attained a certain quality. My personal favourites among some of the longer established vineyards include Lamberhurst Priory, Wootton and Pilton Manor in Somerset, and Carr Taylor in Sussex, but if you have a local wine do give it a try. Many of the vineyards welcome visitors during the summer, and if you have never had the opportunity of visiting a vineyard abroad, this is a splendid way to see just what goes on.

'British' wine is not the same as English wine, but is made from imported and reconstituted grape must and is a purely artificial fabrication. The advantage is that the concentrated must attracts a much lower duty rate than wine and consequently British wines are cheaper than any other wines.

EASTERN EUROPE

Eastern Europe is a hotchpotch of wines. Most of the Iron Curtain countries produce wine in some quantity. Indeed Russia is the fourth largest wine producer in the world, with Romania in sixth place. However, it is Yugoslavia, followed by Hungary and Bulgaria that make the greatest impact on our wine consumption.

AUSTRIA

The wines of Austria have closer affinities with Germany than with her Eastern neighbours. Some of the same grape varieties are used, such as Rhine Riesling and Müller-Thurgau. Her wines have generally less acidity and higher alcohol than the wines of Germany, as a result of Austria's warmer climate.

In the southern Tyrol, vines are trained along arbours to expose the ripening grapes to maximum sunlight.

The most typical Austrian grape, that accounts for a large part of her production, is the Grüner Veltliner, which is peculiarly Austrian and from which are made simple wines best drunk when young.

YUGOSLAVIA

Yugoslavia produces a varied collection of vines and wines, almost as varied as the different cultures and languages that make up the country. The most commonly found Yugoslav wine in Britain is Laski Riesling. This is not the same grape as the Rhine Riesling of Germany. It is quite a different species that can also be called Welschriesling or Italian Riesling. Lutomer Riesling is also common and is a Laski Riesling produced at Lutomer in Slovenia. The general style of Laski Riesling is slightly sweet, quite fruity, without a lot of distinctive character – in other words, rather bland, very easy to drink and goes with everything, but very boring if you had to drink it every day.

HUNGARY

Hungary also produces Olasz or Laski Riesling in large quantity, but it has two other claims to wine fame – Bull's Blood and Tokay.

Tokay is legendary; it is usually a sweet wine, of varying degrees of lusciousness. The sweetest is called Tokay Essencia and then there is Tokay with a number on the neck label, from two to six, to indicate the degree of sweetness. Szamorodni describes the unsweetened version. Tokay Essencia is accredited with all kinds of life-restorative and aphrodisiac powers, but it is now extremely rare.

Bull's Blood is a traditional red wine which has now also become a recognized brand name with some commercial significance. Its name comes from a sixteenth-century legend which suggested that the wine gave the Hungarians unlimited strength against the invading Turkish army.

BULGARIA

Bulgarian wines are beginning to make an impact in Britain. They use western European grape varieties, and are labelled according to the name of the grape rather than any region. The local grapes are also interesting; try Cabernet Sauvignon and Mavrud in red and Chardonnay in white.

THE EASTERN MEDITERRANEAN

GREECE As a new entrant to the EEC, the wines of Greece are likely to become more common in Britain, especially as viticulture and production methods in this fairly backward part of Europe are gradually modernized. The most typical wine is Retsina, a white wine flavoured with pine resin.

Another interesting wine is Samos Muscat, from the island of Samos and the Muscat grape. Well chilled, it makes an unusual dessert wine. For basic table wine, the Demestica brand is quite reliable, if unexciting, for both red and white.

CYPRUS Cypriot wines are worth trying. The industry is controlled mainly by large co-operatives, making wines under brand names. Legends about the goddess of love abound in Cyprus, so Aphrodite is an appropriate name for a medium-dry white; Othello is good for red and there is also a sweet, sticky dessert wine, Commanadaria, named after a crusading order of knights.

LEBANON While in the eastern Mediterranean, mention must be made of a pioneering Lebanese who, against incredible odds, has maintained a vineyard and produced wine without interruption in the Bekaá Valley. Serge Hochar of Château Musar makes both red and white wine, from a mixture of French grapes, mainly Cabernet Sauvignon, and following French traditions. The red is better than the white. The red comes under the Château label, and is a wine of considerable quality. However, the basic Cuvée Musar should not be ignored either; it is a well-made wine of an unusual vigorous character.

THE NEW WORLD

Viticulture and wine-making are very much part of European culture. Wherever Europeans have settled on other continents, inevitably vines have been planted and wine made. Consequently all the former colonies of European countries with the appropriate climatic conditions have developed their own wine industries.

CALIFORNIA

Although wine is now made in several of the North American states, from Texas to Missouri and Pennsylvania, it is really from California that the best North-American wines come. California owes its early wine-making to the Spanish missionaries who

In California in the Napa valley the scenery is idyllic and the vines tended with the utmost care to produce wines of great character. (Right) Young vines at Château St. Jean.

came from Mexico. Of course, in European terms, the Californian wine industry is new, a mere 100 or so years old. The first winery, Almadén, was set up by a Frenchman, Charles Lefranc, in 1853. Then came Prohibition and many wineries fell into disuse or only survived by growing table grapes or by making wine for the Holy Sacrament. Curiously, the revival of the Californian wine industry did not begin in earnest until the mid-1960s, but since then each year has seen the establishment of new wineries, with increasingly modern techniques. Now even the French are investing in California. Baron Philippe de Rothschild of Château Mouton-Rothschild has joined up with Robert Mondavi, one of the pioneers of the Californian wine industry, to make a Californian wine in the style of Bordeaux, and he is not alone amongst the Bordeaux châteaux owners. Champagne houses too have set up operations in California, most notably Moët et Chandon at Domaine Chandon in the Napa Valley.

Grapes grow all over California from Mendocino in the north down to the Santa Ynez valley in the south. The best-known vineyards are in the Napa and Sonoma Valleys to the north of San Francisco, but other important areas include the Livermore Valley to the east of San Francisco and the 500-mile stretch between Los Angeles and San Francisco contains several pockets of vineyards. Finally there is the vast San Joaquin Valley, further inland, which provides grapes for port- and sherry-style wines.

The basic difference between European and Californian wines is that whereas in Europe the precise position of the vineyard is vital in determining the quality of the wine, in California it is the reputation of a particular winery and its wine-maker, as well as the grape variety, that are important. So when buying a Californian wine, look for the name of the winery and the grape variety or 'varietal' as they say in California. Virtually all the

The Sterling winery is at the northern end of the Napa valley.

European 'varietals' are produced in California. The best red is generally considered to be Cabernet Sauvignon and the Chardonnay has adapted most successfully amongst the whites. The basic difference in style is one of alcohol content. The wonderful Californian sunshine produces ripe grapes with lots of sugar, which consequently makes heady, alcoholic wines. There is also a uniquely Californian grape, Zinfandel. Nobody quite knows where it came from and there are various theories, most unsubstantiated, as to its origins. It grows all over California and can vary very much in style, from a light Zinfandel Nouveau to a port-like wine called Zinfandel Essence.

Californian wines have often been criticized for being too expensive, but then so are the best European wines. The wines from the top châteaux in Bordeaux compare in price with what the Californians call their 'boutique' wineries, the small wineries that only produce a few thousand cases a year. However, some of the larger wineries are producing wines that can be found in this country at a reasonable price. Best known of all is probably Paul Masson for his red and white wine in carafe rather than bottle. These are what the Californians call 'jug' wine and over there quite often 'Chablis' for the whites and 'Burgundy' for the reds. They are wines characteristic of the technical expertise which prevails throughout the Californian wine industry. Other names to look out for are Almadén, Christian Brothers, Parducci and Wente Brothers. These are all fairly large wineries that make sound and relatively inexpensive wines. A large variety of wines from the small 'boutique' wineries can also be found over here, but at a price.

SOUTH AMERICA

ARGENTINA is the world's fifth largest wine-producing country and her wines were sold quite widely over here until the

Falklands conflict. Let us hope that her full-bodied reds and perfumed whites, made from European grape varieties, will shortly reappear on our wine merchants' shelves.

It is to CHILE that we must look for South America's best wines, from vineyards in the foothills of the Andes mountains. Reds are better than whites and Bordeaux grape varieties have been introduced with considerable success. Cabernet, Merlot, Sauvignon, and Semillon all do well. The producers to look for are Concha y Toro, Viña Cousiño and Miguel Torres of Spanish renown and the prices are very reasonable.

AUSTRALIA

Wine has been made in Australia for 150 years or so and, unlike California, without any break in continuity. However, it is only over the last 20 years that table wines have come into their own. Previously port and sherry styles, heady dessert wines and Australian 'Burgundy' dominated the country's wine production. Today, however, some superb table wines are being made from European grape varieties.

The most important wine states are New South Wales, Victoria and South Australia, and, to a much lesser extent, Western Australia. The Hunter Valley is the most important region of New South Wales, while the best areas of South Australia are the Barossa Valley north of Adelaide and Coonawarra.

Australian wine-making is a combination of tradition, experiment and enthusiasm. There are distinctive styles for the different areas but, as in California, it is the winery and the grape variety which really determine the choice of wine. Australians also believe in the informative label, and from it you can be told virtually the entire history of the wine, with details of grape varieties, soil, temperature, harvest dates and serving hints.

A 100-year-old vine in the Barossa valley, South Australia.

The Hunter Valley is best known for Hermitage (or Shiraz) in reds and Semillon is the traditional white. Victoria produces a variety of different table wines, including Australia's best dessert wine, made from the Muscat grape. Château Tahbilk, north of Melbourne, makes some excellent reds and Seppelts is another name to look out for.

The Barossa Valley in South Australia owes its origin to German settlers and its wines still retain Germanic characteristics. The leading white is the Rhine Riesling and reds from Cabernet Sauvignon and Shiraz are also good.

However, the best reds of Australia come from Coonawarra. It is the southern-most vineyard in South Australia, with a correspondingly cooler climate, and the reds, especially Cabernet Sauvignon, are subtle and elegant. The best-known of these very good wines is Wynns.

Australia is a wine country with a future, offering refreshing competition to more traditional producers.

New Zealand

The New Zealand wine industry is just beginning to make an impact. New vineyards with European grape varieties have been planted over the last decade or so on both the North and South Islands. Cabernet predominates in the reds, but whites are really more important. Müller-Thurgau is the most widely planted variety, and follows the Germanic style. Rieslings, Chardonnays and Gewürztraminers are to be found too.

SOUTH AFRICA

South Africa, like Australia, was once a prolific producer of so-called port and sherry. These are still made but in smaller quantities and South Africa has made an enormous improvement in the quality of her table wines. This was helped considerably by the introduction in 1972 of a control system for 'Wines of Origin', which designated 14 different areas and defined the use of terms such as vintage, estate and any grape varieties or 'cultivars' as they are known in South Africa.

The heart of the South African vineyards is around the towns of Paarl and Stellenbosch. The wine-making industry is concentrated in the hands of the KWV, a kind of national co-operative with five wineries. There are many other estates producing fine wines, of which Nederburg is the best known, partly for its annual wine auction.

South African wines are full-bodied and rich in alcohol and flavour; they are wines that are warm and gutsy and characteristic of a sunny climate. The main red grapes are Cinsault which has also been successfully crossed with Pinot Noir, to make Pinotage, a warm, berry-flavoured wine. Better are Shiraz, similar to the Syrah of the Rhône Valley, and also Cabernet Sauvignon. Most common amongst the whites is Steen, the South African name for the Chenin Blanc grape. Steen is grapey and fruity.

The climate in the Cape is perfect for vine cultivation.

SPARKLING WINES

The greatest of all sparkling wine is champagne, from a small area of the same name in northern France around the towns of Rheims and Epernay. It was in this area that the special process for making champagne was evolved. It had long been noted that the wines of Champagne tended to develop a slightly fizzy character in the spring; in other words they began fermenting again after the winter cold. It was Dom Pérignon, a Benedictine monk and the cellar master of the abbey of Hautvillers, outside Epernay who, in the seventeenth century, realized that this sparkle could be kept in the bottle by corking it. The process was perfected by Madame Clicquot in the early nineteenth century. This independent lady of character was left widowed (hence the name Veuve Clicquot) in her early twenties to run her husband's firm. She invented the process of *remuage*, a procedure to remove from the bottle the sediment caused by secondary fermentation. The bottles are placed in racks, or *pupitres*, on their sides and gradually moved every day over a few weeks so that finally they are vertical but upside down and all the sediment is resting on the cork. The neck of the bottle is then frozen and the sediment, within a plug of frozen wine, is removed (*dégorgé*).

This is the basis of the Champagne method that has been imitated in many other parts of France, as well as in other countries of the world. A still wine is made in the normal way, usually from black Pinot Noir grapes, as well as white Chardonnay grapes. Then a measure of sugar and special yeasts is added.

(Left) Sulphur is sprayed over the vineyard in early summer to protect the vines against oidium (powdery mildew), a serious fungal disease. (Right) Casks in the Moët et Chandon cellars containing the finest champagne of the house.

The yeasts react with the sugar to cause a secondary fermentation, and the wine is left to mature for a minimum of two years. The sediment is then removed and another measure of sugar and wine (the *dosage*) is added. It is this that determines the sweetness of the champagne from Brut, Extra-sec and Demi-sec to Doux. Some champagne has no wine-and-sugar at all and this is very dry indeed.

Champagne is a blended wine made from wines from many different vineyards within a small area. Each champagne house owns some vineyards and buys additional grapes from the growers. Their aim each year is to produce a wine that is characteristic of their own house style, be it a lighter or a richer wine, and for this purpose they keep supplies of wines from previous years to add to the blend. It is only in the very special years that a vintage champagne, with wines purely from that vintage, is made.

There are some 19 *grande marque* champagne houses, with names like Bollinger, Krug, Veuve Clicquot, Moët et Chandon and so on, but in addition much champagne is sold as BOB wine – Buyers' Own Brand. This is the jargon term for wines made to the requirements of special customers. For instance, several wine merchants and supermarkets have their own champagne. Often these wines are cheaper because they do not have to bear the cost of advertising, but this does not at all mean that they are inferior.

The question must be asked, what makes true champagne unique? After all, the method of production is now copied all over the world, so it must be the special combination of grapes and soil in this small part of France that gives champagne its individual flavour, for it does have a taste quite unlike any other sparkling wine. Its name is protected and it is only outside Europe that it is possible to find 'champagne' that is not proper champagne. In America, for instance, any sparkling wine is called champagne.

But what of the other sparkling wines that are made by the *méthode champenoise*? Saumur, on the Loire, is an important centre for Saumur Brut and Crémant de la Loire and there are close affinities between these wines and those of Champagne. Sparkling wines have been made in the Loire Valley since 1811 when Jean Ackerman, the son of an Antwerp banker, arrived from the Champagne area, where he had been studying their production methods. His marriage to a Mademoiselle Laurence, the daughter of a vineyard owner, marked the founding of the company Ackerman Laurence, the first house to make sparkling wine in Saumur. Their method is identical to the champagne method, except that Chenin Blanc, the main white grape of the Loire Valley, is used. Other important houses include Bouvet Ladubay, Langlois Château and Gratien Meyer; the last two have very close links with two champagne houses.

Elsewhere, there is Crémant de Bourgogne, either from the vineyards around Chablis, or from further south in Burgundy, and several houses in Alsace now make Crémant d'Alsace. One sparkling wine in France claims to be even older than champagne and that is Blanquette de Limoux. It is made from local grapes near the southern French town of Carcassonne by a variation of the champagne method and has a crisp, fruity acidity. Better known are two sparkling wines from the Rhône Valley – St Péray in the northern Rhône and, further south, Clairette de Die – which comes in two forms: Clairette de Die Brut, that is using the pure champagne method with the Clairette grape, and Clairette de Die Tradition. 'Tradition' indicates the use of the Muscat grape to make perfumed wine, and the method of achieving the sparkle is slightly different: the bubbles are the result of one fermentation rather than two.

(Left) Remuage *in the cellars of Veuve Clicquot, the Rheims champagne house where the process was first devised.*

France also produces a lot of sparkling wine that is not made by the champagne method, but by another called *cuve close* or the Charmat method. This should be quite clearly indicated on the label. The essential difference between the two methods is that whereas for champagne the second fermentation takes place in the bottle, for the *cuve close* method it takes place in a sealed vat. In other words, the difference is one of scale. Instead of the need to remove the sediment from each bottle individually, the contents of the vat can be filtered under pressure, so it is very much cheaper to produce. The best-known brands are Veuve du Vernay and Kriter, but there are lots of other French *vins mousseux* or sparkling wines around.

The champagne method has been carefully imitated in northern Spain in Penedés. The town of San Sadurní de Noya, near Barcelona, is the centre of the industry and the home of the main producers of Cava, the name for Spanish wines made by the champagne method. Again, the only difference is the use of regional grape varieties. Freixenet and Codorniu are the two best-known names, but there are several others.

Italy also makes sparkling wine, both dry and sweet. Most famous is Asti Spumante, made from the Muscat grape, by the *cuve close* method. The good ones can be deliciously luscious; the bad, artificial and sickly. However, in recent years there has been an increasing trend in Italy to make dry sparkling wines, using either the champagne or the *cuve close* method. These wines can be found throughout Italy and *spumante* is growing in popularity among the wine-makers of Italy.

Germany is the home of Sekt. The production method may be either that of champagne, but more commonly of *cuve close*, or indeed a variation of the two called the transfer method, whereby the second fermentation takes place in bottle, but the wine is decanted into a vat so that the sediment can be filtered away under pressure, and the wine is then rebottled. Simple Sekt is unlikely to have been made from a grape of German origin, for Sekt producers import still wine from Italy and France to turn it into sparkling wine. If the label says 'Deutscher Sekt' the product is entirely German; if it says 'Rhine Sekt' or 'Mosel Sekt' or gives some other geographical definition, then again the wine comes from that area alone.

Outside Europe sparkling wine is made in California, South Africa and Australia – either by the champagne or the *cuve close* method. But a word of warning before you open a celebratory bottle. There is a great deal of pressure inside a bottle of champagne, so when you are opening any bottle of sparkling wine, do not inadvertently point it at anyone, because the flying cork with its metal top could cause injury. Opening the bottle with a loud pop may be fun, but the extra bubbles (or *mousse*) which froth out are a waste of good wine. The *mousse* will be easier to control if the bottle is chilled first for one or two hours. Gently twist the cork, not the bottle, to ease it out, and have a glass ready to catch the bubbles.

FORTIFIED WINES

Wine is fortified by adding grape brandy at some stage during the production process. The exact procedure varies from wine to wine.

Greatest of all fortified wines are port and sherry, but the essential style of these wines has been imitated in several other parts of the world. Enjoyable but less common are Madeira and Marsala, and there are other wines more of local importance, such as Malaga from southern Spain and the various *vins doux naturels* of southern France.

PORT

English merchants in Oporto in the eighteenth century played an enormous part in the development of the port trade, and today many of the famous names in port have an English ring.

Oporto in northern Portugal is the centre of the port trade. The vineyards are on the steep terraced hillsides of the river Douro. There are some 80 different varieties of vine which struggle for survival in the poor soil and extremes of temperature with harsh winters and scorching summers.

The production of port begins like that of any other red wine. The juice is left to ferment on the skins for several days so that the maximum amount of colour, fruit and tannin can be extracted. Grape brandy is then added when the fermentation is nearing completion, and finally the wine is aged, according to the type of port it is destined to be.

Although there is some white port produced (it can provide an interesting alternative to sherry, as an aperitif), it does tend to be rather expensive. The most commonly available ports are ruby and tawny. Ruby port is a young red port that has been aged in wood for a minimum of two years and is blended from the grapes of several vineyards and from different years. It is young, rich and warming. Tawny is also a blend of years and vineyards. Cheap tawny port may also be a blend of red and white port, but fine tawny port has been aged in wood until its colour has changed from ruby red to tawny. It usually carries an indication of its ageing period – 10, 20, 30 or over 40 years.

The traditions of the Englishman's wine have evolved around vintage port, which like champagne is made only in the very best years. The wine is bottled about two and a half years after the harvest and then left to mature in a quiet cellar for at least 15 years. This is a very small and specialized part of the port trade.

Those of us who enjoy the style of vintage port, but are less patient, can content ourselves with Late Bottled Vintage, or LBV as it is commonly called. It comes from one good, but not vintage, year and is aged in wood for three and a half to six years before bottling.

Although port is basically a blended wine, several of the port houses do occasionally make a wine from a single vineyard or *quinta*. This may happen in a year that is not otherwise declared as a vintage. Port is *the* drink for a winter's night. In England we tend to drink it after dinner, sometimes with Stilton cheese or walnuts. The best-known port shippers include Taylors, Fonseca, Dow, Warre, Cockburn, Sandeman and Croft. Often their ruby and tawny ports are sold under brand names. Port-style wines are also found in other parts of the world; in California (where it is called 'port') and in Australia and South Africa (where the name 'port' is protected and it can only be called 'tawny' or 'ruby').

SHERRY

Sherry is a white wine that ranges from very dry to very sweet. Its home is the southern Spanish town of Jerez de la Frontera – the name sherry being the anglicized version of Jerez. Sherry has long been appreciated in this country, and English mer-

From the Douro valley barcos *bring barrels of port down river to* Oporto, *centre of the port trade.*

(Above) Sherry production: adding alcohol to the must.

(Top) Pressing grapes to make Madeira in Funchal.

chants have also played their part in the development of the sherry trade. Harveys, Sandeman and Duff Gordons are famous names alongside Gonzalez Byass and Domecq.

Sherry is a blended wine. Its basic character comes from the Palomino grape that is grown on the chalk soil around Jerez. However, it is the blending of the wine that determines the end result. The young wines are sorted into categories of quality and style and accordingly put into a *criadera* or 'nursery'. From the *criadera* the vines move into the *solera* system, a process of blending that depends upon a young wine taking on the characteristic of the older wine. When some mature wine is drawn off from a barrel, the barrel is topped up by a younger wine. Needless to say, only a small percentage of wine can be taken off at any one time, and as there are several stages to a *solera* the whole process can take many years, and yet the wine will always taste the same. The *solera* sherries are then sweetened and strengthened with alcohol as required.

The driest of all sherries is Fino. This takes its individual character from a form of yeast called *flor* that develops on the surface of the wine. This is one of the rare instances when contact with oxygen is beneficial to a wine, because the yeast thrives in air. Fino is delicious chilled, and is at its best when young and fresh. Once the bottle has been opened, keep it in the fridge.

Manzanilla is a variation of Fino which, some say, has a distinctive salty tang. Amontillado comes next in ascending order of sweetness. The best are old Finos that have become heavier and richer with age. In practice it is more usually a medium-sweet blended sherry. Oloroso is richer, sweeter and darker still, and forms the basis for sweet cream sherries, that are warm and brown and can be deliciously nutty. For the lovers of sweet sherry who consider it not quite the thing to profess to any enjoyment of sweet wine, there is Pale Cream sherry. Palo Cortado is a rarity which, in taste and character, is almost a cross between a Fino and an Oloroso. Although sherry is out of fashion at the moment it should not be neglected. A chilled Fino on a summer's day, or a warm Oloroso on a winter's night, are a delight.

Sherry is made in other countries. However, the name of sherry is protected to the extent that the country of origin must be clearly marked on the label next to the word 'sherry', so 'Cream South African sherry' is permissible, but not 'South African Cream sherry'. South Africa makes the best imitation of Spanish sherry, with methods and styles similar to those of Spain. Cyprus is another important producer of 'sherry', using less sophisticated methods than in Spain with less distinguished results. British 'sherry', like British wine, is the product of reconstituted grape must which has, as often as not, originated in Cyprus.

Madeira

The volcanic island of Madeira, some 400 miles off the coast of North Africa, is an autonomous part of Portugal and it has given its name to a fortified wine that had its heyday in Victorian times, but is now neglected. Madeira cake was so called because it was considered the ideal accompaniment to the wine.

As well as being fortified, the *estufa* process – in which the wine is heated for four to five months at a temperature of about 49°C (120°F) – is vital to production of Madeira, giving it a distinctive caramel tang.

All four styles of Madeira are long-lived wines. Sercial, the driest, makes an interesting aperitif. Verdelho is a little fuller and richer. Bual is more of a dessert wine, with a medium-sweet flavour. The famous Malmsey is a rich, warming after-dinner drink.

WINE-BASED COCKTAILS

Cocktails add zip to any party, and wine is an ideal basis for many recipes. Use a reliable table wine rather than a vintage example and sparkling wine instead of champagne. Sugar syrup (right) is an easily made basic component.

Measure the quantities carefully and use a large mixing glass. In a shaker, use crushed ice and do not fill it more than half way.

SUGAR SYRUP

Makes ¼ pint/150ml
¼ pint/150ml Cold water
2oz/50g Granulated sugar

Place water and sugar in a saucepan and heat gently over low heat, stirring occasionally, till sugar dissolves.

Bring to the boil, then remove from heat and leave to cool before using.

(Note: sugar syrup can be stored in an airtight container in the fridge for several weeks.)

Madeira Sangaree

To serve 1
2-3 Ice cubes
¼ pint/150ml Madeira
1 teasp/5ml Icing sugar

Place the ice in a wine glass.
  Add the Madeira and icing sugar and stir thoroughly.

Sherry and Vermouth

To serve 2
2-3 Ice cubes
¼ pint/150ml Dry sherry
2½fl oz/65ml Sweet vermouth
2 dashes Angostura

Place the ice cubes, sherry, vermouth and Angostura in a mixing glass and stir well.
  Strain into a wine glass and decorate with fruit.

Sherry Refresher

To serve 1
4 Ice cubes
2 Orange slices
1 Lemon slice
¼ pint/150ml Dry sherry
1fl oz/30ml Sugar syrup (see page 78)

Place the crushed ice cubes and slices of orange and lemon in a tall tumbler.
  Add the sherry and sugar syrup and stir thoroughly until combined.

BUCK'S FIZZ

To serve 3
1/4 pint/150ml Orange juice
    (unsweetened)
1/2 pint/300ml Champagne

Pour the chilled orange juice
into 3 champagne glasses or
flûtes and top up with the
chilled Champagne.

BLACK VELVET

To serve 1
1/4 pint/150ml Guinness
1/4 pint/150ml Champagne

Carefully pour the chilled
Guinness and chilled
Champagne together into a
tall glass, tumbler or tankard.

CHAMPAGNE CUP

To serve 6
1 Bottle of Champagne (80-
    81cl)
2fl oz/60ml Brandy
2fl oz/60ml Curaçao
1 fl oz/30ml Maraschino
1fl oz/30ml Grand Marnier
2 teasp/2 × 5ml Icing sugar
Ice cubes
1 Sliced orange
6 Strawberries

Place chilled Champagne,
brandy, Curaçao, maraschino
and Grand Marnier in a
punch bowl or large jug.
    Add the icing sugar and ice
cubes and stir well.
    Serve over ice in glasses,
decorated with fruit.

SANGRIA

To serve 6-8
1 Bottle of red wine (75cl)
4fl oz/120ml Brandy
12fl oz/350ml Fizzy lemonade
8 Ice cubes
1 Sliced orange
1 Sliced lemon
1 Sliced lime

Place the red wine, brandy and chilled lemonade in a large jug or punch bowl. Add ice cubes and pour into glasses.

Spear the sliced fruits on to cocktail sticks and use to decorate each glass.

RED WINE COOLER

To serve 4
12 Ice cubes
1 pint/600ml Red wine
¼ pint/150ml White rum
2½fl oz/65ml Sugar syrup (see page 78)
2 tbsp/2 × 15ml Orange juice (unsweetened)
2 tbsp/2 × 15ml Lemon juice
Soda water
4 Lemon slices

Mix all ingredients, except soda water and lemon slices, in a jug. Pour into tall glasses. Top up with soda water and decorate with lemon.

CLARET REFRESHER

To serve 3-4
4-5 Ice cubes
¾ pint/450ml Claret
½ pint/300ml Lemon juice
Soda water

Crack the ice and place in a shaker with the claret and lemon juice.

Shake well until thoroughly combined then strain into large glasses and top up with soda water to taste.

CLARET FLIP

To serve 1
2-3 Ice cubes
3fl oz/85ml Red wine
1 Egg yolk
2 teasp/2 × 5ml Sugar syrup
   (see page 78)

Crack the ice and shake well
in a shaker with the wine,
egg yolk and sugar syrup.
   Strain into a glass.

WINTER WARMER

To serve 4-6
1 Bottle of red wine (75cl)
2fl oz/60ml Orange juice
   (unsweetened)
4fl oz/120ml Port
2fl oz/60ml Brandy
2 tbsp/2 × 15ml Caster sugar
10 Whole cloves
2 Cinnamon sticks

Heat all the ingredients very
gently in a saucepan for 15
minutes, stirring
occasionally. Serve warm in
heatproof glasses.

CLARET CUP

To serve 4-6
6 Ice cubes
1 Bottle of claret (75cl)
2fl oz/60ml Maraschino
1½fl oz/40ml Curaçao
2 teasp/2 × 5ml Icing sugar
1 Sliced orange
1 Sliced red apple

Place the ice cubes and claret
in a large jug.
   Stir in the maraschino,
Curaçao and icing sugar and
mix.
   Decorate with orange and
apple slices.

VERMOUTH COCKTAIL

To serve 1
2-3 Ice cubes
2fl oz/50ml Dry or sweet vermouth
3-4 dashes Orange bitters
1-2 dashes Angostura
1 Strip of orange peel

Place the ice cubes in a mixing glass. Add the vermouth, orange bitters and Angostura.

Stir well, strain into a glass and decorate with a strip of orange peel.

MEDIUM MARTINI

To serve 1
2-3 Ice cubes
½fl oz/15ml Dry vermouth
½fl oz/15ml Sweet vermouth
1fl oz/25ml Dry gin

Crack the ice and place in a shaker with the vermouths and gin.

Shake well then strain into a glass and decorate with a cherry.

(For a Dry Martini omit sweet vermouth; for a Sweet Martini omit dry vermouth.)

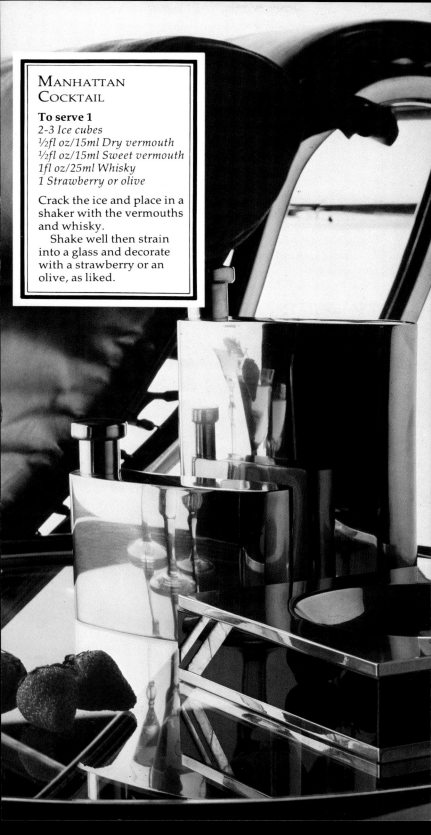

MANHATTAN COCKTAIL

To serve 1

2-3 Ice cubes
½fl oz/15ml Dry vermouth
½fl oz/15ml Sweet vermouth
1fl oz/25ml Whisky
1 Strawberry or olive

Crack the ice and place in a shaker with the vermouths and whisky.

Shake well then strain into a glass and decorate with a strawberry or an olive, as liked.

KIR

To serve 1

*½-1 fl oz/15-25 ml Crème de
  cassis or blackcurrant syrup*
3fl oz/85ml Dry white wine

Place the crème de cassis or
blackcurrant syrup, in a
glass.

Top up with the chilled
white wine.

RHINE WINE PUNCH

To serve 18-20

6 pints/3.5 litres Rhine wine
*1 pint/600ml Sparkling mineral
  water*
2fl oz/60ml Brandy
3fl oz/60ml Maraschino
8oz/225g Icing sugar
2 tbsp/2 × 15ml Tea leaves

Place the chilled wine and
chilled water in a punch bowl
with the brandy, maraschino
and sugar. Add the tea leaves,
tied in muslin. Remove after
10 minutes and stir well.

SAUTERNES PUNCH

To serve 8
2 × 75cl Bottles of Sauternes
1fl oz/30ml Maraschino
1fl oz/30ml Curaçao
1fl oz/30ml Grand Marnier
Seasonal fruits

Chill the bottles of wine thoroughly.

Place chilled wine, maraschino, Curaçao and Grand Marnier in a large jug or punch bowl.

Decorate with a selection of seasonal fruits.

WHITE WINE AND COINTREAU

To serve 2-3
½ pint/300ml Dry white wine
2½fl oz/65ml Cointreau
3 Ice cubes
½ pint/300ml Soda water
Orange slices

Place chilled wine, Cointreau and ice cubes in a mixing glass; stir well and strain into 2 or 3 glasses.

Top up each one with chilled soda water and decorate with orange slices.

RHINE WINE CUP

To serve 4-6
1 Bottle of Rhine wine (70-72cl)
1fl oz/30ml Curaçao
2fl oz/60ml Maraschino
1 teasp/5ml Icing sugar
4-5 Ice cubes
Pineapple pieces
Orange slices

Place the chilled wine, Curaçao, maraschino and icing sugar in a large jug. Add ice cubes and stir well.

Serve in glasses, decorated with fruit slices.

Peaches and Wine

To serve 10-12

1 Bottle of still Moselle
(70-72cl)
1 Bottle of sparkling Moselle
(70-72cl)
3 Ripe peaches or
14oz/400g Can of sliced
peaches
1-2 tbsp/15-30ml Caster sugar

Chill the wines thoroughly. Peel, stone and chop fresh peaches, or drain and chop canned peaches, and place in a large jug or punch bowl.

Add ½ the bottle of still Moselle and leave to stand for 20-30 minutes.

Stir in the remaining chilled still wine, the sparkling wine and sugar.

Port Wine Cocktail

To serve 1
2-3 Ice cubes
2½fl oz/65ml Port
1 dash Angostura
1 dash Orange bitters
3 dashes Curaçao

Place the ice cubes in a
mixing glass with the port,
Angostura, orange bitters
and Curaçao.
   Stir well and strain into a
glass.

Port Refresher

To serve 2
2-3 Ice cubes
¼pt/150ml Port
2½fl oz/65ml Cointreau
*1 teasp/5ml Icing or caster
   sugar*
4 Olives
2 Cucumber slices

Crack the ice cubes and place
in a shaker with the port,
Cointreau and sugar.
   Shake well until
thoroughly blended then
strain into glasses. Decorate
with olives and cucumber.

Port Flip

To serve 1
2-3 *Ice cubes*
2½fl oz/65ml Port
1 Egg
2 teasp/2 × 5ml Icing or caster
sugar
1-2 pinches Ground nutmeg

Crack the ice cubes and place
in a shaker with the port, egg
and sugar.

Shake well until
thoroughly combined then
strain into a glass and add
nutmeg to taste.

GLOSSARY

acidity sourness giving a lively taste to a wine.

aroma the smell of a wine before being matured in bottle.

balance an acceptable combination of the important elements in a wine: alcohol, acidity, tannin, fruit and sweetness.

bloom a faint white coating on grape skins which contains a high proportion of wine yeasts.

body the amount of alcohol, sugar and soluble solids in a wine.

bouquet the characteristic smell of a mature wine.

chambré (French) brought to the temperature of an unheated room – about 15°C (60°F).

champagne method (French – *méthode champenoise*) a way of making good-quality sparkling wine, following the way in which true champagne is made.

chaptalization a process in which sugar beet is added to must to provide the yeasts with extra sugar to be transformed into alcohol.

claret red wine from the Bordeaux region.

corked/corky having an unpleasant, musty smell – most likely because of a bad cork.

crisp (of white wine) refreshing and with an acceptable.

cru (French) literally, 'growth': used to indicate several categories of quality, e.g. *grand cru*.

cuve close **method** (French) a method of making sparkling wine in which the secondary fermentation takes place in a sealed vat.

dry lacking in sweetness.

finish the aftertaste of a wine. A good-quality wine has a long finish.

flabby having too little acidity.

flinty another word for 'crisp'.

fresh having a young taste or smell and an attractive degree of acidity.

heavy having too much alcohol and too little acidity for the levels of fruit and sugar. Sherry, port and any other wine with an alcohol content of over 15% fall into this category.

hock a German wine sold in brown bottles, from Mittelrhein, Rheingau, Nahe, Rheinhessen or Palatinate.

light having a delicate flavour. The term applies to wines with an alcohol content of less than 15%.

maderized another word for 'oxidized', applying mainly to white wines.

mis d'origine, mis en bouteille à la propriété (French) estate bottled.

must freshly pressed grape juice before fermentation is complete. Must sometimes contains grape skins and pips, depending on the type of wine to be produced.

nose the bouquet of a wine. In addition, 'to nose' a wine means to swirl it around in a glass and then to sniff it in order to appreciate it fully.

oxidized having been exposed to the air for too long. An oxidised wine lacks brightness, has a tarnished colour and a flat, stale taste.

pétillant (French) very slightly sparkling.

rich luscious and full-bodied but not necessarily sweet.

secondary fermentation this is when malic acid is transformed into the gentler lactic acid by the addition of sugar and special yeasts. This process reduces a wine's acidity.

sparkling having small bubbles (containing carbon dioxide).

star-bright completely clear

steely having a lot of acidity.

tannin a natural preservative from grape skins, pips, stalks and wooden casks. It has an unpleasant taste reminiscent of stewed tea.

'tears' (or **'legs'**) clear liquid falling slowly down the inside of a glass after a wine has been swirled around. Very noticeable 'tears' are produced by wines with a high alcohol content and vice versa.

transfer method a method of producing sparkling wine in which the secondary fermentation takes place in the bottle, but for less time than that allowed for champagne. The wine is then removed from the bottle, filtered under pressure and returned to clean bottles.

vinification wine-making.

vintage (a) the wine made from a season's grape harvest; (b) the season when grapes are picked for making wine; (c) the harvest of grapes during a particular season; (d) a vintage wine is one made only from the grapes harvested during a particularly good year.

viticulture the growing of grapes.

weight another word for 'body'.